MANAGING
How to survive a

CW00621612

PATRICIA ('PADDY') O
years at Southampton Ar
yoga and runs a personnel t
programmes on stress management, women's development and time management. Paddy O'Brien is married
with four children.

Overcoming Common Problems Series

Overcoming Common Problems Series

Overcoming Common Problems Series

Overcoming Common Problems

MANAGING TWO CAREERS

How to survive as a working mother

Patricia O'Brien

SHELDON PRESS
LONDON

First published in Great Britain 1989
Sheldon Press, SPCK, Marylebone Road, London NW1 4DU

British Library Cataloguing in Publication Data

O'Brien, Patricia
    Managing two careers: how to survive as a working
    mother (Overcoming common problems)
    1. Great Britain. Working mothers. Practical
    information
    I. Title II. Series
    305.4'3'0941

    ISBN 0–85969–588–3

Typeset by Deltatype, Ellesmere Port
Printed in Great Britain by Courier International Ltd, Tiptree, Essex

Contents

Acknowledgements

I would like to thank all the women who discussed their dual career lives so frankly in order to share their insights with other women in the same situation. I am grateful for specialist advice from Julia Pokora on training matters and from Tim O'Brien on tax matters and financial planning. Margaret Greaves, author and psychotherapist, used the title 'Managing Two Careers' for a workshop at Southampton University, and kindly let me use the title for this book. Thanks to Brenda Tomason for the typing. Tim, Jon, Ben, Dan and Zoë were terrific, as always.

1

Women with Two Careers

This book is for any woman who cares about her work, cares about her children, and is attempting to live a life that includes both.

It is an invitation to share in the experiences of many women trying to do just that, and hear of their hopes and fears, their dilemmas, compromises and working solutions.

It is also an invitation to drop the façade of a glittering smile and an insistence that 'everything's fine', and instead to get down to exactly what the issues are. Most of the women in this book have had, are having, something of a bumpy ride, but are candid enough to say so in the belief that the best way forward is for us all to pool our ideas and support one another, rather than put pressure on one another, and make one another feel inadequate, by suggesting that we have everything under control.

Laura stood at the front door saying goodbye to her ten-month-old son before setting off to an important meeting at a prestigious management college. Slowly and thoughtfully he vomited over her tailored suit. 'Nothing I can do to help' said her husband, sweeping off to *his* work. There she stood, like so many of us have, before and since – faced with managing her two careers.

No two jobs, no two women, and no two children or families of children, are the same. In this chapter four women in very different professions talk about their decision to try a dual career option, and help us get our subject into focus. They describe their feelings about their decision during pregnancy, and shortly after the birth. They tell us what the pitfalls have been for them, and pass on material they wish they'd known before they tackled the situation.

First is Caroline:

I'm a midwifery tutor in a midwifery school in a large teaching hospital.

It's full-time and a very responsible job. We're training the midwives of the future there.

I never doubted for a moment during my pregnancy that I would return to work. Actually my own mother put quite a lot of pressure on me to stay at work; I think she was frustrated with her own life and didn't want to see me sink into domesticity. I was confident about going back right up to the birth – I had my baby in a different hospital from the one I work in because I wanted to be well away from my colleagues then! The birth was lovely, really easy.

A few weeks after my daughter was born I was if anything even more determined to go back to work. She was a crier. She cried so much during the first three months of her life that at times I was at my wits' end. I had to shut the door of her room sometimes and go downstairs and put the television on loud just to get ten minutes' respite. Unfortunately, when it was time to go back was just when she had got over all her colic and crying, and was becoming a really nice little person, smiling, cooing, and playing delightfully.

Nevertheless, I stayed with my original plan. My colleagues were amazed; they had been quite sure I would end up staying at home with her.

I think I do do my job differently now. When I'm teaching about labour I speak quite freely about my own experiences of labour, which I think some of my older colleagues think is terrible – much too personal. In one way it's bad that I had such an easy labour. I probably still don't have any idea what it's like to have a ghastly, complicated and painful labour, and therefore I can't really communicate that to the students.

It took a few goes to get the timing and the travelling right – I go early to miss the rush hour and my partner takes my daughter to the babyminder, and I fetch her at the end of the day. Actually I think it's quite nice for the two of them to get that hour together.

I used to take work home before I had the baby, but not now. If it doesn't get done at work it doesn't get done. I am better organized than I was before, and I do get through more while I am at work. Once we get home I really concentrate on baths and stories and playing – I feel it's my time with her and I don't let anything else distract me. I went on breastfeeding her till she was 18 months – just a little feed early in the morning – I think probably I hung onto that for as long as I did because I was away from her all day.

Two things I would pass on to other women are these. I know what my daughter's routine is at her babyminder's, so when she crosses my mind during the day I can work out what she's probably doing, and that feels very important to me.

Secondly, I made friends at antenatal classes with a pregnant archaeologist who was also keen to go back to work after her baby was born. We gave each other terrific support – we used to meet but also we used to ring each other up any time it was all getting on top of us – even when we were both back at work we used to call each other at work sometimes to give vent to frustrations or worries or give each other a word of encouragement. It was very important to know someone who was in exactly the same situation, having exactly the same doubts and complications, and going through the same hundreds of slightly different phases as you gradually get yourself organized.

Jill's work is part time, but also pretty high pressure. She says:

I'm a programming officer at a Community Arts Centre and I work 21 hours a week. I'm responsible for booking all the events at the Centre and for liaison and coordination and working with volunteers. It's a cooperative style of work and we have to try to run a balanced programme, but my big personal commitment is to live events.

I saw no alternative to continuing to work. I was positive that (a) I wanted to go on with my job because I love it and (b) I didn't want to be at home all day. That feeling continued right through my pregnancy and after Katie's birth.

In a way it was easier because I never lost the continuum of work: I was not replaced and had to continue consulting with the centre. There was no gap in which I might have started to panic.

When I first physically went back to the office I used to take her with me in a carrycot, but of course that grew less and less practicable. For me the crux of being happy back at work has been getting the right carer for Katie. I think you've got to be *totally* happy about your child or children's carer. As far as I'm concerned she's got to *want* to do things my way.

I've found it hard to organize myself mentally although my mind has not been as divided as I feared. Nevertheless it was a shock to me the first time I realized I hadn't thought about Katie all day. I do have a very supportive partner. He insists that we *both* employ a nanny so that we can *both* do the sort of work we want to.

In my work now I'm a lot stronger. I'm more direct. I don't mess around. I'm proud of the labour I went through, I feel I'm a strong person and have faith in my own personal ability to survive and my mental attitude to suffering, so I'm more able to push through ideas and deals.

I like being away from her for part of the time although I do miss her. Being among adults and in a completely different mental world is important to me, so is being busy, feeling stretched intellectually.

There's lots of advice I wish had been given in those first months so I'll pass it on to other women now.

1. Be totally convinced about your carer for your child; spend a lot of time looking for the right person.

2. Give yourself some time during the day. Don't fill every second. Rest sometimes.

3. Have time in your working life for calm times.

4. Be positive. Don't concentrate on guilt; spend time making life work the best it can. Have the courage to tell colleagues you have, not a problem, but a different way of life because you have a child, and must make your decisions accordingly. If you respect yourself in that situation instead of apologizing for it, they respect you.

Jane was in post-doctoral medical research before her second baby was born. Because of the attitude of her employers, and her own circumstances, she decided to change tack quite radically:

Now I'm working freelance. I write science workshops for infant and junior schools and I'm writing a textbook of workshops. I also work in health education two days a week evaluating the health education programme.

My last contract before the baby was born expired six weeks before his delivery. I thought I'd give myself a year to see if I was happy at home.

The birth of the baby was so lovely that the feeling of joy stayed with me for many weeks and I even looked with some favour on the idea of having a third. Gradually, though, the repetitive tasks, the endlessness of them, made me feel I must do something else as well. I felt grief at losing the world of science of which I'd been part for so long. Four weeks after my son was born I had to go and give a lecture, which reminded me how much I liked being part of science. By three months I knew I was not contented and began to think what I could do. I was not just out of work because of my pregnancy. The state of science funding is such that I might well have found myself out of work anyway.

I seemed to be facing a brick wall. The bricks were: the baby brick, my husband's career brick [see chapter 8, 'Managing Three Careers'], the funding brick. My old team manager was also a brick in this wall, since he said 'People who work part time lack commitment', which shook me to the core. Each one of these things on its own was surmountable, but all piled together they made a formidable obstacle.

I changed my attitude completely after this baby was born. Instead of trying to make my family fit round my job, I had to look for a way to fit the job round the family. I wanted a flexible, mobile work pattern, which is the complete opposite to what medical research wants from you. I used to have a reasonable salary. Now I'm on pennies but I am my own boss and can decide what to do and act on it.

Because of this reappraisal there has been a benefit which might never otherwise have happened. I have found a creative part of myself that I never knew existed.

I'd say to anyone who is wondering how to work her career and her family together: Don't think about what anybody else is doing, you have to evolve your own solution. If it isn't right first time be brave enough to abandon it and try something else; there's more than one way to skin a cat. I was always too rigid before. I used to admire people who were single-minded, but now I see you have to look for different ways to handle different circumstances.

Here are the views and experiences of Laura, who runs her own business:

I'm a management consultant and my background is in psychology. I help businesses to plan and manage the human element of change – it's the 'soft' side of management consultancy.

I always assumed that I would continue to work when I had children; I wasn't sure how I would feel, but I assumed I wouldn't want to stop, and indeed I didn't. Late on in the pregnancy I didn't really think about it any more. I was concentrating on getting the baby born and was focused on that.

A couple of weeks after he was born I thought I would never work again. Actually I felt really quite mentally ill. I was suffering from insomnia and depression; I could hardly get through a day, let alone do any work. I felt very frightened of trying to go back and of the commitments already set up for four or five months ahead.

I just sat it out and endured it and eventually it got better. People pushed me to attend work meetings, which at the time I found very stressful, but I think actually that helped. I took tablets to help me sleep, which sometimes worked and sometimes didn't. I had a very supportive spouse and understanding friends. But really I would say I *evolved* out of it, I didn't *act* out of it.

Once I got back into work, which I do part time, I found I was enjoying it although I did feel torn. I was very wobbly. I still wasn't sleeping so I was still tired. I was anxious about my ability to do the work, in fact about my ability to do anything. I was however beginning to be glad to have some time away from my son.

A year later I would say that now I do my job better than I did before my son was born. I had such a difficult time with the birth and everything afterwards that I am more grounded in myself, which is important in my type of work.

I'm also a bit more laid back; having experienced real suffering I've got a different perspective on difficulties and disturbances in the work context.

The other difference is that I don't now accept work that would take me away from home for weeks at a time, which I used to do before.

I'm very wary about giving advice to other women because my advice would come out of my experience. Having said that I think it's important to get a good nanny or good childcare set up as quickly as possible after the child's born and let them get to know each other as quickly as you can.

If you're self-employed, like I am, you can phase in the timing and build up your time at work gradually.

I'd also say, talk to as many other working mums as you can and get a database from doing that.

And lastly I'd say, keep reviewing whether what you're doing *is* actually what you want to do. Stay in touch with what's right for you and ignore what anybody else says – they're dealing with their own stuff.

In spite of the range of fields they work in, all these women emphasize the importance of originality, flexibility, and independence of spirit. While we wait for industry and institutional employers to catch up with the major bank that has begun to provide workplace nurseries for employers, and to respect that a career break does not mean a person is not serious about her work, we have to be inventive about the pathways our careers may take.

Furthermore, even when every workplace has a nursery there

will still be work to be done on the emotional factors for parents and child on separating for part or all of the 'working' day, and careful consideration given to where one's energies are going and where one's centre of gravity really lies.

In the following chapters we shall look at the essential elements that need care, creativity, logic, and good planning applied to them in the enterprise which many of us will undertake at some point in our lives, of managing two careers.

2

Managing to Delegate

Good delegation is vital for any woman who has two careers. It's an important part of trying to recognize clearly that you are telescoping together two activities, either of which could easily spread to take up your entire time and energy. Think over the alternatives to good delegation. How often, for instance, have you stood at the supermarket checkout in your lunch hour, your blood pressure doubling every 30 seconds, as you grow later and later for an afternoon session at work, and get into a worse and worse state to deal with it when you finally do get there? How often have you staggered in through the front door at 5.30 into a messy, chilly house, the breakfast plates congealing in reproachful heaps and the children brawling? The nuisance and disappointment of buying things unwisely, disastrous and unsuitable choices of clothes and food, are often the result of hasty shopping crammed into minutes in the middle or at the end of the day. Missing deadlines, dental appointments, library return dates; these are all often the result of an overcrowded timetable and an uncertain set of priorities.

Far more dangerous are mistakes we make in traffic because our minds are racing on ahead to the next items on the agenda. Susan describes how she rode her bike straight across a crossroads, right into the path of an oncoming car: 'Part of me knew I had to stop, but part of me just went on riding automatically because I was so engrossed in what I was going to do when I got to work. In some very fundamental way I forgot to look after myself.' Susan and the car managed not to collide, but she and the driver were both very shocked.

Driving over red lights, not assimilating the situation properly at junctions, or reacting slowly because of over-tiredness, are all factors we should face up to as consequences of over-commitment.

Women also report from time to time a panicky sense of

dislocation experienced when they are trying to cram too many activities and responsibilities into their day. Jill said: 'I stood in a Southampton precinct and thought 'What am I doing here? What did I come into town for?' I couldn't remember what I was doing and why, or even where I'd left my car. I thought "This is nature's way of telling me to slow down!" '

How easy, and ultimately, how dangerous it is, to think we can somehow do all the childcare and the housecare, round the edges of our 'real' work. We *can* exist like this for a while, but we shall burn out in a matter of months if we do. Our strategy for survival has to include first of all a realistic assessment of what we want to delegate. After that it's a question of thinking through what you could delegate to other members of your household, and what you are going to have to pay for somebody else to do. When you have come to some conclusions about those there may well be a nasty residue of things you can't get rid of! The secret with this is to look for ways of minimizing the time and effort you have to put into things which you really would rather not be doing.

How much can you delegate?

Try taking stock of all the work you are doing at the moment. Make two lists: firstly a list of all the jobs you do at work, and secondly a list of all the jobs you do at home. Yes, *all* the jobs. Don't miss out emptying the dustbins, doing the packed lunches, redecorating, feeding the gerbil, organizing social events at work, or preparation and thinking through or work issues that are done at home. Do you help children with homework, or friends or partners to prepare work or study? Do you take the telephone messages or add up the books? Do you give regular lifts to clubs and sports centres to others, or have regular weekend commitments with relatives? Write it all down and have a good look at your lists. Their relative lengths may give you some information at once about where and how much you might like to begin planning to delegate.

In addition to your two lists, make a calculation as to how many hours a week you spend in paid work, and how many in unpaid work. Also, add up roughly how many hours a week you spend having fun. Include as fun anything you find relaxing and enjoyable – anything that 'takes you out of yourself'. Write the results of your calculation down. Do these numbers reflect the kind of balance you want in your life? Maybe they do – if so, that's a positive thing to find out and feel pleased about. Many women, however, find a staggeringly high number of hours in the 'unpaid' column, and a sadly tiny number of hours for 'fun'. In a group of women workers recently we tried this exercise – and after a bit of discussion several women said they had artificially lowered the 'unpaid work' number because they felt if they put the true number down it would look as though they felt sorry for themselves! In some cases the true numbers in the totals were as high as thirty or even forty hours of unpaid work per week.

In groups where the women were a mixture of women living in partnerships and women living alone or still with their parents, another striking point emerged: the high number of hours of fun the unpartnered women had compared with the others. Instead of being embarrassed about what a hard time they were having, they were tempted to lower artificially their thirty or thirty-five hours a week of fun! We laughed about it a lot together and teased these women about their hedonistic lives, but many of the partnered women muttered darkly about the horrors of marriage or co-habitation, and said they would be careful to pass the information we'd discovered on to unpartnered daughters.

Having any chance to reclaim some opportunities for 'fun' depends very much on setting up a good system of delegation.

To return to the issue of unpaid work, the least we can do for ourselves, even if we find we can't offload any of the labour, is to notice ourselves doing it. Statistically speaking, the unhappiest people in modern Western societies (in terms of tranquillizer dependence, admissions to mental hospitals, suicide attempts, etc) are women who do only unpaid work, i.e. women whose sole employment is childcare and housecare. It is because the work has no proper name, no pay and no status, but is repetitive and exhausting. In cultures where homemaking and childcare are genuinely shared, respected, and supported, this adverse effect is not seen. We can begin to take care of ourselves and each other in this respect by paying proper attention to this work.

Armed with your two lists of 'jobs at home' and 'jobs at work', mark with an asterisk the jobs you would like to delegate. Don't at this stage worry about who on earth you are going to delegate to, just assess what you would like to be rid of. Go through the 'home' list first. If you are faced with a plethora of household tasks, consider keeping any that you find some attraction in. Do you enjoy, for instance, the hot fragrance of a pile of ironing, or bringing up a glow on the wood by smoothing polish into furniture, or do you get satisfaction out of cooking lovely meals? If you do, consider keeping those, and think about delegating the tasks that really make your heart sink.

Now look at the 'work' list. Consider what your strengths and prospects at work are, and hang onto anything that enhances your sense of being good at your job, and your prospects of progressing. Consider delegating anything that bogs you down unnecessarily. Julia, for instance, hated parts of her job that involved running a particular computer programme which she found decidedly un-user-friendly. She delegated this element of her work to a colleague, and concentrated more effort into the areas where she was working more strongly and successfully. You may want to delegate mechanical or administrative tasks, or negotiate with colleagues over clients for whom you would like to exchange responsibilities – it depends on the nature of your work, and where you feel your strengths lie.

With both your lists now marked with asterisks, begin to consider action. On the 'home' list work out which of the jobs could appropriately be delegated to another member of your household. Write down whom, and decide when to discuss it with them! Think about how to talk about it assertively, rather than aggressively, or in a spirit of aggrieved martyrdom! Work out clearly what your proposal is, and make it directly to the person you need to negotiate with. Try not to pad it out. 'Padding' is the flood of words we tend to produce when we feel anxious or lacking in confidence. Often it takes the form of compulsive apologizing (as one woman said: 'When someone treads on my

11

foot, *I* apologise!). 'I'm sorry to bother you about this now . . .' 'Would you mind awfully if we talked about this. . .' 'I know you'll think this is silly, but . . .'; this is all padding and you can do without it. Take a deep breath in, and as you breathe out, breathe the urge to apologize away. Then try: 'I would like to talk about sharing the ironing', or 'I would like to re-organize the shopping and cooking – could we discuss it?', or 'I would like to fix a time when we can sort out who does which jobs at home'. Avoid resentment or hysterics because a calm, direct approach is more effective in getting results in this kind of negotiation. If you *feel* resentful and hysterical, make sure you get a chance to get it off your chest later though; perhaps with a trusted friend!

If you are getting children to join in housecare, show them slowly and carefully how to do the task you are going to assign to them, and then accept their best shot at it. Don't undermine their efforts by 'finishing off' for them, and don't forget to say if you appreciate their efforts.

One more point about sharing chores: see how it feels if you avoid using the word 'help'! 'My husband's very good, he helps in the house', always sounds strange since it's his house too and his shared responsibility; and if children join in, for instance, in preparing a meal, they aren't really helping, because they're going to eat it too – they're participating. When we say and think 'help' we are still caught in the assumption that it's still *really* all our work. Unpicking simple bits of language can be liberating!

Look at what is still on your list marked with an asterisk and think about whether these are tasks you might be able to pay someone else to do. Do you have enough money at this point to pay someone else to take over some of your unpaid work? Could you divert any money that you are spending a bit fruitlessly at the moment, to free yourself from some of these tasks? Would your partner or other members of your household split the cost? Find out what the local going rate for domestic work is, and if you decide you want to employ someone, advertise at a local newsagent or in the local paper. Always ask for references.

Many women have complicated feelings about paying some-one else to do 'their' cleaning work. They fear that they are exploiting the women who they employ, and also that they are somehow 'cheating' by asking somebody else to do the work for them. These ambivalent feelings cannot be smoothed away in a glib fashion. It *does* feel complicated to pay a low hourly rate to another woman to do work you hate doing yourself. You are, however, at least making a payment for a type of work which, as we've said, is so often unacknowledged by payment. Ideally, you might find someone who enjoys the work and has a flair for it that you might not have, and who wants the hours in the area where you live. In the best possible case, it is an arrangement which benefits you both.

Lastly come the bits of work you have no suitable candidate for delegation for. If you have an uncooperative partner, or are bringing up your children single-handed, and do not have much money, this may be your largest category. Can you minimize the boredom and exhaustion of the tasks you want to delegate by pairing up with someone else to do them? A joint assault on the supermarket or launderette can be less tedious than a solitary one. (If you are a single parent feeling isolated, it might be useful to get in touch with Gingerbread or Spinoff). Minimize the effort required for weekday food if possible by having lots of salads, fruit and cheeses, and fill up with baked potatoes and wholemeal bread. When you buy clothes for yourself and children, bear in mind ease of care, and aim to have as many things as possible that need no or minimal ironing. Keep one space wherever you live pleasantly tidy for yourself to relax in in the evening – otherwise limit yourself to one big clean and tidy up once a week. Exchange ideas with other people as to how to streamline housework and try not to worry about 'cheating'; value yourself and your own well-being more than sparkling skirting boards.

Think over what you need to take on your 'work' delegation list. Arrange meetings with colleagues with whom you want to negotiate. Anything you want to subcontract, note down, and decide when to make the necessary phone calls and enquiries to get estimates and arrangements fixed up.

Look at the list of items at work that you would like to delegate but can't see how to get rid of. Can any of these items be cut right out? If so, let them go. Are some of them activities you dislike because you don't feel well enough trained or prepared for them? Would you benefit from further training to give you more confidence and expertise in that area? If so, make an appointment with your boss to discuss the matter. Otherwise work out how to cut down the effort going into these tasks, or allocate one block of time per week to them so that they don't seem to dominate your working life.

Delegating childcare

Delegating part of the care of our children is the major step most of us take when we decide to or have to have the dual career of motherhood and work. It is the most important bit of delegation, and the most highly emotionally charged. Whether the person we share childcare with is a relative, a childminder or a nanny, we need a person we can trust and empathize with. It may be useful to start looking for someone while you are still pregnant, rather than struggling with the ups and downs of the first weeks with a new baby and trying to sort out childcare arrangements at the same time. Think over the alternatives before your baby arrives. Try not to panic – everyone's emotions go into a turmoil initially at the thought of being separated from their baby or child. Angela said:

In the first few weeks when I went back to work after Amy was born my dream life was very disturbed. I kept dreaming about losing Amy. In one dream I went to a conference and took her with me in my briefcase. I was a bit uneasy about her being in the briefcase but felt she'd be basically all right. Then at the end of the day I set off home and I had picked up the wrong briefcase, and someone else took mine with the baby in it and set off somewhere in an aeroplane. I felt helpless and despairing.

Her anxiety about separating from her baby shows clearly in the dream. We should also remember that in the early stages our babies are presumably going through something similar, and we and our babies need to help and support each other while getting into the rhythm of separating and coming together again.

14

It may also help to remember that ours is the first generation of women ever to assume that being shut in a house for 24 hours a day with our offspring is the natural condition of motherhood. Previous generations had the give and take of an extended family to spread the childcare around, and a safer environment. Those of us over 30 remember with some amazement how we 'played out', riding tricycles on the road in quiet cul-de-sacs, and playing on the pavements unsupervised for hours. Traffic was less heavy and less hazardous, and children, even very young ones, did not need to be shut indoors. Also there was, or seemed to be, far less danger to children of assaults by strangers. The nightmare of child abduction, rape and murder seemed far away in those days, and although the child of very careful parents I was allowed to go with friends to play in the woods for hours on end even at the age of five or six. Thinking of letting our children do that in this day and age makes our blood run cold. Children have to be kept in or in sight all the time, and this increases the isolation and pressure on mothers. In not wanting to spend all our time with our children we may be more rather than less in tune with what mothering has always involved.

You could employ a nanny who will come to your home and care for your children, or a childminder to whose house you would take your child or children. A childminder may also be looking after children from other families.

You can find nannies by finding a local nanny agency in the Yellow Pages or by checking local colleges to see if they have a nursery nurse training course, or you can advertise yourself. Interview candidates carefully – clear your mind beforehand and decide what kind of person you are looking for. Write a clear and careful job description and negotiate properly if you want to make any changes in the duties and programme later on.

To get a list of childminders contact your local Day Care Social Worker at the Council. Make a short list, then visit the prospective childminders in their homes. Don't rush. Be clear with yourself whether it is an environment where you will be happy for your child to spend a great deal of time. Discuss any special points you want to make about diet, potty training, general discipline and so on. Again, write down clearly an agreement between the two of you about how many hours a week you want her to work for you, how much per hour you will be paying and how often (weekly? monthly?), and anything else you want to spell out clearly.

Let the baby or toddler get to know the nanny or childminder gradually by making visits together, then leaving them for an hour or two at first, building up confidence and the relationship between the two of them, until you gradually bring the hours up to what you want.

Never take your nanny or childminder for granted – remember she needs positive feedback as much as anybody else. Show you appreciate her important work. Never arrive late to collect children without ringing first (and only then if it's unavoidable), or pile on extra hours without proper consultation and agreement.

Sometimes relations living nearby will offer to look after your baby when you go back to work. This can be marvellous but the groundrules must be carefully worked out and mutually agreed if the arrangement is not to break down in recriminations and misunderstandings.

Bear in mind the school age children need care after school and at half terms and holidays until you feel they are mature enough to spend some or all of those periods independently.

Working out the groundrules carefully at first, and keeping honest and assertive lines of communication open, are the key points in keeping the balance in delegating childcare. There may be problems you haven't forseen. Laura was puzzled after interviewing the young women who applied to be her son's nanny. Two candidates were very good, and of these two one was highly recommended and particularly skilled. Eventually, after some honest heart-searching, Laura chose the second person, who was not quite so expert and a bit more ordinary, because the first person, the more obvious choice, made her feel a bit inadequate. She felt a novice at the skills of motherhood and did not want to be overwhelmed by a super-nanny. She did ring the unsuccessful candidate up and explain in a light and assertive way the reasons for her decision, and that candidate soon found another job.

Her feelings bring to our attention that we may feel threatened sometimes by our children's alternative carers. It's important to discuss these feelings with a friend you trust and not bottle them up. The worst time for me on this issue was when two of my children called their childminder 'Mummy' for a few weeks. I felt they had completely written me off, although on reflection I would guess it is more likely that they were trying to express their confusion and be quite sure what the differences between us were. Even though they were only two and three years old I told them it made me fed up and sad and they stopped (although they still pretend to mix our Christian names up for a joke, so they are obviously still working away in their own minds as to how interchangeable we really are!) If our children spend many hours a day with a person who isn't us, they will have a strong and, we hope, a loving relationship with that other person as well as ourselves. The one does not exclude the other.

When you have assessed what you need to delegate and set it all up, decide how frequently you should monitor the different areas: weekly, daily, monthly, whatever. Then the last bit is also up to you. You've made a lot of effort to cut down the *angst* in your life, so make sure you really do get the benefit of it by, when you have delegated something, stopping worrying about it and *really* letting it go.

3
Managing Time

To begin to use our time better, we first need to recognize that time is a resource, just as fuel or food or money might be. In the cliché 'time is money' it even becomes a commodity although that does seem a particularly harsh approach. For a woman with two careers the priority would seem rather to work away from time being an enemy and towards time being a flexible and manipulable medium.

The Eastern approach to time holds an interesting contrast to our own. The prospect of several incarnations in which to achieve whatever one's potential is in the world certainly takes pressure off activities in any particular lifetime! It's intriguing that the final arrival at peaceful nirvana is defined as freedom from time. However, coming across the epigram in a yoga textbook 'he who practises headstand for three hours a day overcomes time', I could do nothing but snort in modern Western derision.

Our Western culture has 'played' with time in the form of the highly complex theory of relativity. Inaccessible to those of us without higher maths except through paperback 'guides' such as the Fontana *Modern Masters* series (and possibly *The Hitch-hikers Guide to the Galaxy*!) this gives an uncomfortable feeling that time is not linear as most of us experience it, but elliptical and simultaneous. Again, fascinating though it is, my vague grasp of the theory of relativity has not consoled me when I have missed a train or tried to be in two places at once. I simply experienced what one dual career mother vividly described when realizing she should have been somewhere else at that very instant collecting her child: 'Oh God, if only I could sprout wings!'

Whether time is elliptical or linear, whether you feel you will have many incarnations or just the one, try looking at how your time is spent at the moment. Find the analysis of your time that you made in chapter 2, or if you have not done the analysis yet see page 9 and work your figures out.

Be effective, not busy

The dread of being suspected of neglecting your household, coupled with the dread of being suspected of not pulling your weight in your working environment, tends, all too often, to encourage you to overwork all round. Your children's T-shirts are all freshly ironed and your reports are always filed (or whatever), up to date, just to convince everyone you won't fall short of what they would expect of a single career person. Here I think it's very useful to reflect on this remark in a paper on management training: 'It's the easiest thing in the world to be busy – what's difficult is to be effective'. It's difficult not to build up a whirlwind of hectic activity around ourselves to convince ourselves and everybody else that we are achieving terrific amounts. This activity, intended to stem our anxiety, actually feeds it. It's helpful to work on *not* trying to be credible by being astonishingly busy, and *not* automatically believing in other people's credibility just because they're astonishingly busy: it may well be that rather than being important and productive, they just aren't managing their time too well. You can be giving 100% without feeling dreadful – or to put it another way, if you feel all right, that doesn't mean you've been lazy. The quantity of tasks that need doing is large when you're holding down a job and running a family, but it's up to us to select, organize and prioritize our work so that it's manageable.

A further myth I was relieved to explode in a quiet corner with a friend, is the myth of 'quality time' with children. For a number of years I heard 'working' (outside the home) mothers justifying their separation from their children by saying 'I don't spend quantity time with them, but I do spend quality time'. After a glass of wine I confided to this friend that I did not feel my time with my children was quality time at all – it was just time, sometimes good, sometimes bad, less of it than if I was a full-time mother, more of it than if I was absent, ill or dead. To my joy she agreed and said that she felt just the same way, and we laughed slightly hysterically at having come out of the closet. If your time with your children is *always* unpleasant, obviously you need to try to work out why, but if it has its ups and downs, it's unlikely that there's anything too awful going wrong. It's perfectly all right if it isn't all cosy chats or joyful excursions.

So, cut some things out or cut them down if you are suffering from overloading, particularly in both categories of 'unpaid work', and look at the self-nourishing aspects of hobbies and fun. As far as cutting down goes, look at chapter 2, 'Managing to Delegate', as a great deal of agony can be removed from life by some wholehearted and specific bits of delegation. Next, cast around your friends, colleagues and your own imagination for any ingenuity that may help you cut down. Not having overcome the ironing fetish myself yet, for instance, I am really impressed by people who have. Marilyn, mother of two and a community worker in a deprived inner-city area, describes her decision never to do ironing again and her system simply of putting clothes in the drier when she's around to take them out as soon as it stops, and hanging them straight onto hangers or folding them onto shelves. 'My son didn't know what an iron was when they showed him a picture of one at nursery school', she said. 'He thought it was a kind of boat'. Just think of it.

Take time out

Part of your planned time every day should include some time doing nothing much: a minimum of 30 minutes each day, outrageous though that may at first seem. A man whose partner left him trying to hold down a demanding job and look after three children told of his initial decision never, ever to do less than two things at once to get through his in-and-out-of-the-house work load. Six weeks of intense effort like this left him for months in a state of physical and emotional collapse. In an emergency we can all, of course, rise to a level of multi-competence we cannot expect of ourselves normally. The adrenalin we generate in a crisis enables us to carry through simultaneously activities, any one of which in a calm moment would rob us of all composure, but there is a price to pay for this: a deep mental and physical bleakness experienced once the immediate danger has past. Readers of *Nella Last's War* (highly recommended to all women everywhere) and many other diarists and correspondents of the Second World War will be familiar with this on a grand scale – the almost limitless resourcefulness and goodwill under pressure, and the bleakness and anomie once the tautness of crisis is removed. There is a real physiological risk (documented, for example, in studies of hostages' experience) of living life as if it were a permanent red alert, and becoming addicted to the flow of one's own adrenalin. One needs to make a conscious decision not to live that way, not to let one's self-esteem depend on living that way, and to build doing-nothing-much into one's day to avoid the fate, in emotional terms as it were, of spent knicker elastic.

How this 30 floating minutes is spent is of course a matter of convenience, money and opportunity. It might be 30 minutes soaking in a fragrant bath – not trying to read, not trying to work anything out, not focusing on future plans. It might be half an hour gazing from the window of a train or bus, letting someone else do the navigating and driving, and not using the time to improve yourself in any way, or it might be sitting, stunned, in front of a slice of mindless, undemanding soap opera. You might be messing around in a swimming pool or a sauna or pottering in the garden or having a leisurely walk round the park or common, so long as it has nothing whatever to do with getting fit, getting thin, improving your knowledge, or being a better person in any way whatsoever. There has got to be some 'give' somewhere in everybody's day. People lose the art of dawdling, and gazing and going into a pleasant semi-trance, not because they have no time but because they lose firstly the knack of doodling around doing nothing and secondly the sense of how valuable it is. If you need convincing, think over how often the solution to a knotty problem has come not through acute concentration alone, but through alternating acute concentration with breaks.

The other element of time to call your own is a spot of at least

30 minutes each day doing something that makes you happy. This may be the same half hour you spent 'doing nothing much'; it's perfectly OK for those two to duplicate each other. Have you forgotten what 'being happy' is? It's not unusual for working women under tremendous pressure to grimace ironically when this point comes up: 'Oh, happiness, yes, I remember that'. It seems to be part of the dual-career guilt package to let one's own innocent and small happiness go in the welter of effort and organization. Don't. Please don't. What is all the struggle for if there are no small oases of spontaneous happiness?

First of all, sort out what makes you happy. What do you personally enjoy, what sweetens your day? For many women there is some disentangling to do here about whether what makes you happy is what your mother or partner or friends or children feel ought to make you happy, or whether your particular thing is ideologically OK or sufficiently respectable or right on. Do you find it hard to admit how much you love knitting or pressing flowers or watching Coronation Street? Please don't. It might not have the street cred of going to karate classes or an encounter group, but if it makes you happy, hang on to it. I love wandering round the chain shops in my lunch hour composing unaffordable outfits in my head. Not even interesting out-of-the-way little designer shops, but High Street chains. This is not what intelligent women are supposed to do with their time, but I cannot find the appropriate scorn in my head. For me, considering how an olive skirt at Marks and Spencers might go with a cotton sweater at Top Shop and silver ear-rings from John Lewis is real time out, however trivial and unworthy anybody else thinks it is. Have a small patch of time every day, whether in grand passion, watercolour painting, shopping, or magazine reading, that gives you some real joy.

Two more issues should be considered before you are ready to start reorganizing your time. First, are there any times when you are supposed to be in two places at once? And secondly, are there any times in your day when you are too exhausted to move? These are both obstacles to getting a good flow of time management.

First, being in two places at once cannot be done. Hard though it is one has to accept it. Women do so often apparently achieve the impossible that it becomes tempting to feel one can do it, or ought to be able to. You cannot walk on water, and you cannot be both at work and at the school gates, both in a traffic jam and at the babyminder's. Repeatedly, working through time management exercises, women working both in and out of the home set themselves this particular impossible task and introduce all sorts of extra distress into their day. Nichola said:

'I felt so mixed up about leaving my children (aged four and two) with a childminder that I used to chronically underestimate the time I needed to get there. I allowed only 10 minutes to get from there to work and only 10 minutes to get from work to pick them up, even though it took a good 15 to 30 minutes each time, depending on the traffic. I was always late everywhere and always tense on that drive, but I really think it was a kind of penance for leaving the kids at all. It's taken me a long time to learn to take them along to their minder a bit earlier and pick them up a bit later. I pay for the extra time in money, but all three of us are in a better state, and I am beginning to think perhaps I don't have to suffer in that way for the privilege of going to work.

Second, when you are so tired you can't move, and want to or do collapse in tears, it's an emergency signal from your whole being, and it is important to listen to it and respond to it, and not be tempted to over-ride it. In the long term you need to tighten up planning and actually cut your workload. In the short term, until you can implement that, the methods of abdominal breathing and basic meditation described in chapter 5, 'Managing Emotion', may help you. When one is in distress there are two problems – how to get through till lunch time, and how to get through the rest of your life. The healing effects of short effective relaxations might pull you through till lunch time, but it's reorganizing patterns and structures that can help you get through the rest of your life.

In the Forces, arduous training often includes an item called a 'sickener'. Participants are told an exercise ends at a certain place only to find when they get there that they have to go on for another mile, exhausted and demoralized. This is supposed to build character. My guess is that all women managing two careers recognize the feeling: thinking you have done all the tasks for the day, only to find an emergency precipitates a need for one more effort. You have to push through that wall of exhaustion and carry on. If we have nothing else in common with the paras we have that, the difference being that their toughness is renowned and ours isn't. Perhaps we can begin simply by acknowledging it in each other.

Time planning

Every day, try making a list of what you plan to do. There is a helpful mnemonic for time planning that spells out the word SMART: Specific, Manageable, Achievable, Realistic and Time-targeted. Somewhat tautologous, it nevertheless gets the main points across. Don't put 'change the world' on your list unless it's a realistic prospect that you might manage it that day. Try out instead putting 'work out how to change the world' and then narrowing it down to the particular piece of world you want to change first. This is how the most apparently grandiose plans can work. The Women's Peace Movement began with the apparently impossible rubric to persuade by peaceful means world powers to disarm themselves of nuclear weapons. By carefully considering specific tasks, cooperative and loving behaviour, and mutual support they have, I believe, created a real force for change and a really different style of organization. A large-scale aim like theirs should not be discounted just because it's so extensive, but the working through of the vision has to be in small, specific steps.

Time-targeting is a commitment with yourself on when you aim to do the thing you're planning. On a daily plan, you may want simply to put morning, afternoon or evening. The basic point is to tie the planning to a specific time so that it does not recede ever more into the future, like the fitness programme that starts next Monday and then because you're too busy never happens, or the reorganizing of the files or the briefcase waiting vaguely for 'until there's a moment'.

When you have included all the things you have to do and all the things you would like to do the next thing is to *prioritize* the list. Take into account two factors, one relating to the items and the other relating to you. Relative to the items on the list, many of them may look very pressing, clamouring to be done first. Sort out whether you feel they are *urgent* or *important*. *Urgent* matters need dealing with because they need quick attention – *important* matters have long-term consequences that you care about. If something is both urgent and important it has to go to the top of the list! Otherwise, trying to give the important rather than the urgent things priority is well worth while. Always delegate urgent things if you can and always keep a hand on the important ones. It always helps to see the wood for the trees. The distinction is more than semantics: it means that you manage matters that are mechanical rather than crucial, but you keep in touch with your long-term aims.

When prioritizing your list consider your mood. If you feel shaky or tired or demoralized put the easiest things first, the more difficult things later. That way you get the confidence that comes from a few successes before you take on the tougher assignments. If you feel energetic and positive, take on the harder items while you still have plenty of good positive energy; water the geraniums and so forth at the end of the day when you're tired. Jill said 'It's a good idea to see those two alternatives. I always felt if I didn't tackle the really difficult stuff straight away I was being a real wimp. It's interesting to think you might not have to be an Amazon all day long to be doing a good job.'

If you're lucky enough to have a job where you can take initiatives about how to plan your day, try to plan in changes of pace and flavour that keep the mixture interesting. If your job is one that is monotonous in itself or is always responsive to other people's needs, it is only your own inner landscape and rhythm you can control, but you can try to get in touch with that and adjust it to how you would like it to be. (See chapter 5 on 'Managing Emotion'.)

The martial arts like t'ai chi and aikido, which eventually teach a very swift but very relaxed response, begin all their techniques with the inner thought 'there's plenty of time'. Contact release dancing, spontaneous and exuberant, start its flow with the thought 'there's nothing to do here'. By looking at time and not being afraid of it we may be able to arrive at a state where we look at the clock not with a sharp intake of breath, but with a true feeling 'there's plenty of time'.

4

Managing Money

Although some of the glossy women's magazines now carry a regular financial page, an intelligent interest in money management seems to be one of the last things to become attractive to women. The Stock Market and the bulk of business and government money have been predominantly managed by men for so long, and private money has also been in men's hands. Although generations of women have long been skilled in ingenious budgeting of 'housekeeping', some of us still fight shy of trying to make major financial decisions, or take real responsibility for money, or understand financial institutions. Certainly some sections of our mothers' generation thought it was unfeminine to try to comprehend financial affairs, and a flair for extravagance was considered rather a disarming quality. This is obviously not appropriate if we're seeking to be taken seriously as equal people, any more than a grown man's inability to sew on a shirt button feels like appealing helplessness in this day and age.

Going back to working outside the home means you have your own money, perhaps for the first time for a number of months or years. Having an independent income gives many women a real sense of themselves as powerful individuals again. It's a good time to review and update your relationship with money.

The 'credit trap'

Buying things, shopping, acquisitive behaviour, is central to many people's lives in the late twentieth century. Consumerism affects us all, the seductive power of money in its most obvious form being its capacity to buy us the clothes, machines, furniture and cars that we desire – or anyway think we do. We are perhaps the first generation of women to have the money ourselves to buy major items, and many of us have fallen headlong into the 'credit trap'.

With minimal accreditation most of us can now get credit cards with high credit limits for many major shops, and also general credit cards such as Barclaycard, Access and Visa. All of them tempt us, as the advertising slogan runs, to 'take the waiting out of wanting', by buying immediately on credit. The excitement and power of ownership can be overwhelming.

There are points in favour of having one or more credit cards. One is that you can, in effect, get eight weeks' free credit, as long as you buy your goods at the beginning of one month and pay for them *in full* by the end of the next. It may be useful at times to take advantage of this. Another point is that the cards are flexible and convenient: they don't need to be pre-arranged like a bank loan, and the general credit cards can be used in most shops for most kinds of goods. If you need an expensive winter coat, you can buy it at the beginning of the cold weather on your credit card if you need to. If yours is the sole source of income in the household, you will find a credit card useful for replacing consumer durables. When the washing machine packs up, for instance, it is an expensive and miserable business saving up for a new one, and a great help to be able to flourish the piece of plastic and pay slowly.

However, the arguments against credit cards are fairly pressing. Instant spending power is expensive: the annual percentage rate of interest (APR) for most cards is between 20% and 30%. If you buy an item at £500 (paying £100 back monthly) (*a*) you can't buy anything else on credit for the next 5 months, and (*b*) the total cost, including interest, will be around £560. The £60 is the cost of borrowing, and you should decide that you are choosing to pay this at the outset.

Can you be sure your credit card won't burn a hole in your pocket? Will you be safe, if you're a bit depressed, from the temptation to spend money to cheer yourself up, when all too often credit card and money don't feel 'real'? Will the glossy presentation of household goods, clothes, records, books, and so forth, overwhelm you? If you're the sort of person who stands in a shop with the voice of reason going on in one ear ('you don't need a new camera') and the voice of rationalization in the other ('it will work out cheaper in the end, and with a holiday *and* a wedding coming up, and what's the point of doing all that overtime if I never have anything decent for myself?'), credit cards are probably a hazard for you. Only take out credit cards if you're really sure you can use them in a decisive and controlled way.

Having less time to wander round shops may protect dual-career women from some of these temptations, but mail order shopping, moving up-market all the time, is often available on a credit system. Again, check the APR on the repayment, and decide whether the convenience of immediate purchase is worth that extra money to you.

If you are already deeply in credit card debt, you are in a very worrying situation, and you must try to sort it out. If you can work it out yourself, do. Give up things you can give up, such as cigarettes, alcohol and any other luxury items. Try not to give into the temptation to give up food and live on your nerves and cigarettes; you will undermine your health, both physical and mental, for a long time to come if you do. Arrange to pay off a fixed amount of money per month – but this needs to be an amount greater than the monthly interest charge or you make no impact at all on the actual debt.

If you can't work it out yourself, contact in the first instance the local Citizen's Advice Bureau (find their address and phone number in the phone book), who should be able to put you in touch with someone who will help you reorganize your repayment and your day-to-day expenses, and work out how to get the situation back under control. Don't close your eyes and hope it will go away – it won't, and the stress of being swamped by debt has led people to despair and even to suicide, so take action.

Think also about taking care of yourself emotionally. When we spend compulsively it's because we're feeling deprived in other ways. It's easy to *say* think about how to have a more satisfying time emotionally, and difficult to do, especially without any spare money, but it *is* a factor in debt problems.

Planning your budget

Even if you find you can keep your credit card use under control, you may want to think a little harder about day-to-day budgeting. We'd all like to run our money rather than feel that it's running us, avoiding panics, and avoiding frittering, and getting more positive enjoyment out of any spending power we do have. This is easier with a fixed income than if you are a freelance whose income fluctuates, but even in the latter situation it's important to attempt to plan.

Firstly, project your future income over the next six months or a year. If you're freelance you have to estimate it; be pessimistic, then any good breaks are a nice surprise, but if you have a thin time your system doesn't break down. Now estimate your unavoidable expenses – major bills, mortgage or rents, rates, childcare costs, clothes and equipment, car maintenance, food bills and anything else you have to pay for come what may. If you're self-employed, remember that Income Tax is one of your unavoidable expenses. The safest thing to do is to put 25% of your earnings straight into a separate account, so that when the Revenue ask for it it's sitting there waiting.

If you're left with a deficit there are really only two courses open to you; either to review the essential expenses and look for what you can cut out or economize on, or to look for ways of earning more money. Your income isn't fixed in the firmament and you can be ingenious in finding ways of topping it up. In fact women are good at finding inventive ways of increasing their earning power because they are often accustomed to manage an 'unconventional' career path. The Equal Opportunities Unit of the Industrial Society encourages women to see their broad variety of experience positively and to call it a 'patchwork career' – though Liz Bargh, who heads the Unit, laughs and says hers is more of a 'chequered past'! Our flexibility is an advantage, but be careful to work out the *cost* of any new work you take on (new clothes or equipment, extra travel, energy expended and emotional wear and tear) and be sure it is really worth the extra money in your bank account.

If you have a surplus, allocate and prioritize it. Make sure it goes on things or activities you really want, and doesn't dribble away on a magazine here, a bottle of wine there, and a plethora of minor purchases, unless you positively choose to give yourself leeway in this respect.

To find out where the money in your purse goes to, keep a record of everything you spend for a whole week. If you can stand doing this exercise it's very informative and will certainly make clear if you are in your view *wasting* any money. If you can judge from this calculation how much cash you can afford or would like to manage on per week, then take that amount out and try to make it last. You can improve your cash flow quite a bit by controlling your small-scale spending.

Banks

When you think about where to put any surplus money and where to store your income, you face a huge range of bank and building society facilities from which to choose. Look out for where you can minimize your bank charges, maximize interest on any remaining surplus and maximize convenience in terms of spending.

At the moment there's a great deal of competition in the High Street for the right to deal with your money, so your bank manager should be sensitive to all these issues. Remember when you go to a bank that you are the customer. There is no need for anyone to be intimidated or patronized by her bank manager, so if that happens to you, take your money and your custom somewhere else. If you have the time and energy write to the bank's Head Office and explain why you have moved.

If you want to take a business proposition to your bank marshal your facts first. Make projections of your expenses and prospective earnings. As well as having your facts and figures ready, it may be worth your while to play the game in terms of your own personal presentation. One woman described how she took her idea for her (eventually sensationally successful) enterprise to one bank while wearing a pair of jeans and with her two children in tow. That manager didn't agree to a loan for her to start her business. On her next attempt she left the children with a friend, dressed up, made up, did her hair, and got a loan.

If you do go to ask for a loan think through an assertive approach, and also think through how you will feel if you do meet with refusal, so that you can keep your composure and make a dignified exit if you want to.

Accountants

A Bank Manager provides banking and credit services. When do you need an accountant? You need an accountant in the following circumstances: if you are self-employed, or a very high earner, or if you run your own company, or if you've got a lot of inherited wealth. Choosing an accountant may be a matter of either asking around for a personal recommendation, or look in the Yellow Pages and ring a few up, to see whether you like the sound of them (do they sound competent, organised, friendly?) Judging their performance is difficult because the work they do for you is often fairly technical. The criteria you can use to make an assessment would be whether the technical functions are being acted on – are they getting your returns in on time and so forth; do you get timely replies to your letters (more than a month's delay is too much). Your work will be delegated from the partner to someone on the staff, but they should give you a person who is your consistent point of contact. If they fail to do this, go somewhere else.

An accountant can help you with your tax returns, tax planning and accounts. Generally speaking accountants are not experts on investments and pensions, but should understand the basic structure of investments and pensions, and your needs in this area.

Tax

If you are an employee your earnings will be subject to PAYE tax deduction at source. The Revenue will issue you with a coding which gives you any allowances due and taxes any otherwise untaxed income (e.g. car benefit from your employer). The resulting net allowance is then divided by 12 or 52 and given as tax-free pay against your monthly or weekly income. It is always worth checking this coding, as mistakes are frequently made and can be costly. You can get information about tax allowances etc. from your local tax office or from any firm of accountants.

If you are an employee, the only expenses that are deductable against your income are those incurred 'wholly and necessarily in the performance of your duties'. The Revenue interpret 'necessarily in the performance of' very strictly; it is rarely worth pursuing a claim unless it clearly satisfies this test. Travelling to and from work, childminding expenses and the cost of any work-related course you choose to go on are three common examples of expenses they consider *not* to be incurred 'wholly and necessarily in the performance of your duties'.

If you are self-employed you need to go to an accountant. She or he will ask you to keep records of your allowable expenses; for instance, you may be able to claim part of your phone, heat and lighting bills if your place of business is your home. If you use your car for business travel you should be able to claim some maintenance and running costs, and some capital allowance against the value of your car. If you need special clothing for your work you may be able to claim against it, but the case of Mallalieu v. Drummond went all the way to the Lords in a woman barrister's attempt to claim allowances against the black suits and white shirts she bought and cleaned solely for court wear. The judge finally threw the case out on the 'dual purpose' clause since she had to travel to court wearing something, and so, he claimed she was 'using' the clothes not 'wholly and exclusively' for the purposes of work.

You can claim tax allowances against publications relevant to your work, and for many other expenses in addition to those mentioned here, of which your accountant will advise you.

On Schedule D there is a time lag of between 12 and 24 months before you pay the tax on your income. This is an advantage if your income is rising because you're paying tax on less income than you're currently earning; the converse, however, applies if your income is falling.

If you are running a business, you may be liable for VAT. If your turnover exceeds around £22,000* per annum, you must register with the Customs and Excise and make a return to them each quarter. If you register late there is a 30% penalty and the Customs and Excise enforce this very strictly. Rumour has it that they will accept death (your own) as a reasonable excuse for *not* getting registered promptly. Nothing much else will do.

Pensions

Most companies have their own pension scheme. All these schemes are now transferable without major penalties. You get tax relief on pension contributions. Generally it is beneficial to join the scheme, because your employer contributes to it.

If you are self-employed, or if you want to opt out of your firm's scheme and take out a personal pension, consult an independent financial adviser. Make sure your adviser is a member of FIMBRA, and rely on her or him to check out the track record of the pension company.

In a pension scheme you, through your pension plan or your company, pay money into a fund which is invested, and the tax-free income from this investment comes to you when you retire. Usually you can choose to have a pension or to have a lump sum on retirement and a reduced pension. The very long cycle of the investment protects the value of your pension against all but the most devastating stock market crash.

Savings

Unless the economy is highly inflationary, there is no need to spend surplus money to preserve its value. You can save in a Deposit Account in a bank, or in a Building Society; generally speaking, the Building Societies offer a better rate of interest. National Savings lends your money to the government rather than the bankers. The National Savings Investment Account is one of the very few kinds of savings not taxed at source, so any

* This figure changes every year in the Budget.

non-taxpayer who has savings can avoid having the income from their savings being taxed at source by putting them into this kind of account.

Investments

If you have a large surplus of money you might want to invest in shares. Playing the stock exchange is a sophisticated and risky form of gambling. The chairman of the Stock Exchange recently said that you need a minimum of £50,000 'to play with' before investing in the Stock Market would *not* be a risk. For most of the 1980s there was a sustained bull market, i.e. the average value of all shares rose; this resulted in an unrealistic belief that investment in shares produced automatic profit. However, the easy money made on British Gas and British Telecom was followed by the débacle of BP, and the general public learned that the market gives no guaranteed results.

The market value of any share fluctuates daily according to supply and demand. Most public companies pay dividends twice a year and their shares' value rises just before and falls just after these. Otherwise the rises and falls happen as a result of rumour of takeover bids, or of events abroad, or a movement in interest rates, or many other things. Very many things affect the value of shares and the stock market can be highly emotional and volatile. If you do want to invest, go to a stockbroker. Choose a broker either by personal recommendation or from the Yellow Pages. You need a minimum of between £1000 and £10,000 to invest, depending on the broker.

Unit Trusts

Unit Trusts are a way into the stock market where you have less money than a stockbroker would bother with. A pool of investors' money is invested in a pool of shares distributed between several companies. With a balanced portfolio the risk is spread. Ask a FIMBRA advisor if you are interested in Unit Trusts – some savers' plans take you into Unit Trusts for as little as £20 per month.

Generally, if you want to know more about money and how it

works, try watching BBC 1's *Money Programme*, to get the basic information.

Lack of money

Although it seems important for all of us to know more about how money works, it is statistically more likely that women will be struggling with poverty than with high finance. Women do two thirds of the world's work but receive one tenth of its income and own only one hundredth of its property. If you are dealing with the DHSS rather than a stockbroker, you are enmeshed in a system even more complex. It would be lovely to say collect such and such a leaflet, put your claim in and everything will be fine. However, as desperate claimants and exhausted and demoralized staff grapple with a system of Gordian complexity, unreliable computers, and often a bad backlog, it is unlikely to be as pleasant and simple as that. Mutual help and support with friends in the same situation may help, but being really poor, or dangerously poor to the extent that your life is about to disintegrate, is a frightening experience that happens to many working mothers at different times in their life. It's certainly happened to me. One vital thing to try to remember is that you are not poor because you are a bad or substandard person, or because you deserve to be poor. Citizen's Advice should be able to help you with the technicalities, and Samaritans are a 24-hour helpline available if you do get to the end of your tether.

A final thought about money – and property in general. If you have struggled and worked for what you own, you might like to make sure it will go to exactly where you choose if you should die. We should all consider making a proper will, by going to discuss the matter with a solicitor and having a will drawn up. You can also nominate in your will the person or people you would like to take care of your children if you should die.

5

Managing Emotion

Pamela trains yachtsmen in marine navigation. After her first child was born she tried to convey to her male colleagues how she felt when she got home from hospital with her daughter, and faced the first few weeks of being responsible day and night for the baby. 'It's like taking a boatload of beginners across the Channel,' she said, 'in fact it's like taking a boatload of beginners across the Channel *every night*.' The similarities are striking – you don't get much sleep and you have to steer very carefully!

In coping with your dual-career existence, managing your emotions, particularly if they are similar to Pamela's taking her beginners across the Channel, can make a vital difference to how you feel you can cope, and to having your energies available for creative effort or fun or being productive rather than burning most of them up in worry or guilt.

Living with our young children we become more vulnerable than we were before. There are specific reasons within the relationship. Firstly, the child's vulnerability and our desire to protect and nurture them winds our emotions up. For many women the sheer power of the love they feel for their children comes as a shock. Having negotiated pre-baby life in a cheerful and happy-go-lucky way, Miriam said: 'I'm amazed to notice that I could cheerfully murder anybody who I thought was going to harm my children. I'm quite afraid of how much I love them.' Also the violence, political instability and personal cruelty we hear and see all the time on the news is not something we can screen off and avoid noticing any more. Alice said:

I'm still hearing all the same things I've been hearing all my life, but now it matters so much more. I cannot bear the fact that we haven't made a world that's a good place for these children to live in; they're so small and so innocent, and there's so much evil and misery in the world. If anything about cruelty to children comes on the television or is in the

36

papers I just walk out now, or turn the page over. I never wanted to read about that kind of thing but since Amy's been born I find it quite unbearable.

Secondly, we don't just attend to our young children through the words they speak, we develop an ability to understand how they are and what they want or need by our observation of their body language. We know very intricately how our child looks and moves when tired, bored, hungry or in need of a cuddle or a change of scene. We're all experts on the non-verbal signals our children give us. I feel that women are highly observant of non-verbal communication anyhow – that our tendency to grow up expecting to be the mediators trains us in sensitivity to atmospheres, expressions and tonal nuances in the voice. I sometimes wonder whether so-called 'feminine intuition' is not an ethereal quality, but rather a lifetime's practice of responsive watchfulness. When our children are born it seems that we gear up that skill in observation even more. What to an outsider sounds like an undifferentiated wail, to the baby's mother will be a clear cry for something specific, whether food, affection or a sleep. This geared-up observation naturally leaves us very sensitive and prone to 'over-react' to briskness or brusqueness in colleagues, clients, whoever we have to deal with, and to feel rather easily bruised.

It may help simply to recognize this increase in sensitivity as a general experience among the mothers of young children (and noticeable in men too if they are spending a lot of time with young children or other vulnerable groups of people), and not a personal peculiarity of yours. It may help to give the feeling a positive name, and not to call it hysteria or instability. Also it may be useful to value what is good about this feeling – that it certainly makes you more human, more humane, more passionate in the wide sense of the word, as in caring about the world, about issues, about people.

Without a doubt, when the two-career life is working well, emotional life is rich and pleasurable. At its best, mental stimulus and adult company at work balance with cheerful times at home, neither world becoming overwhelming or boring. There is little to say about these times except to celebrate and enjoy them when they come along, which, intermittently at least, they certainly do. What we shall look at here is how to tackle the times when our emotions are not in equilibrium, and how to arrive more often at the pleasant state of balance.

To go back to Pamela getting the beginners safely across the sea, one of her experiences there is of sudden crises, such as seeing the lights of a large tanker looming up and having hastily to alter course. Sudden crises lie in wait for any of us attempting to work while our families are young.

Complicated though it may have been, we may feel we have set up the ideal care system for our child or children only to find out the hard way that nannies and babyminders can fall ill just like anybody else, or may need time off for crises of their own. The first few times this happened to me I panicked completely. I felt mentally and emotionally stretched to the limit already by organizing my life. I just could not improvise what to do next. Having been through the experience a few times it occurred to me to make an arrangement between my childminder and another childminder that they would cover each other for sickness, holidays and emergencies, and to get extra help when that meant they were over their limit for numbers. This back-up arrangement has worked well and taken some anxiety out of the situation.

It is also worth thinking what you will do when you are just settled back into work and you go one morning to lift your beloved baby out of her cot to find her smiling at you and covered in spots. Have you worked out how to manage through the inevitable bouts of infant illnesses? If you have a nanny coming to your house, find out which childhood infections she or he has had and is therefore immune to and prepared to work with. If you are taking your children to a childminder you need to sort out the same information, and also the immunities of any other children who go to the same person – although most childhood illnesses are infectious before they 'show', so the children have probably given whatever it is to each other before you even knew it was in the air.

The difficult thing is to work out how best to cope if your child or baby is ill and unhappy because of the illness. This needs good rapport between you and your carer, and some clear thinking on your part. Maybe your child has really a very loving relationship with her other carer and will be as comforted by cuddling from her as by cuddling from you. If so, you may feel you can and want to share the care of your child even when they are ill and distressed, and continue with your work as well. If you have a sense that your baby or child really needs you for a day or a few days, your inner voice may well be right and you should probably listen to it, making whatever contingency plans are necessary at work. Think it through before it happens and try to get clear about your real feelings when it actually does happen. By thinking it through you have a chance to see the options more clearly and make your decisions less hastily. It is an issue that fills most of us with awful guilt and panic, and there are no ideal and simple answers, only more or less useful compromises. Remind yourself that you have a right to make your own decisions and do what you honestly believe is best, and put a shield up between yourself and other people's reactions if they are adverse.

You might want to negotiate with your partner to alternate taking time off for children's illnesses. Also, make a clear arrangement about who should be contacted in an emergency by your children's school or childminder or other carer. Take into account who can reach the child most quickly geographically, and also fair sharing of the responsibility.

Transport can be a source of interesting crises: your car won't start; your nanny's car won't start; the bus doesn't come; the points are frozen and the train is delayed. Anyone doing complicated daily journeys from childminder's to workplace to home and back should consider joining a car rescue service, which at least gives you a back-up if you do break down. Take out the most comprehensive cover you can afford; it will be well worth it, again in controlling your anxiety levels. It is also worth carrying and ensuring that the children's carer carries emergency taxi money in case you get stranded anywhere.

Public transport that doesn't turn up, breaks down or is

delayed is much more out of your control. If it does happen, try to keep yourself in a reasonable state by consciously controlling your breathing and relaxing your muscles. You have to take it half an hour at a time and work out what to do as you go along. It is horrible sitting in a stationary train knowing your children are waiting for you and their carer must be getting anxious about you, but the biggest favour you can do them and yourself is to arrive with them as untensed-up as possible.

Linda pointed out that in coping with her job running the English Department in a large comprehensive school, and taking care of her three children – twin girls and a boy – her skills resembled those of an air traffic controller. She has developed an ability to hold detailed information about all sorts of disparate subjects in her head at once, to be responsible for many different people simultaneously and, to keep a clear head and avoid crashes!

Without a doubt the sheer quantity of information you need to keep available increases geometrically when you combine mothering and work outside the home. You know where the clean pyjama trousers are and how many nappies are left in the pack and how to do your particular work skills and how to negotiate with your manager, as well as remembering to iron tomorrow's blouse and when the car needs an MOT and who needs their measles injection done next; not to mention what to have for dinner and arranging an interview for a new job for yourself. Women groan ironically, 'What I need is a *wife*.'

Holding information mentally at the ready is very stressful: transfer what you can onto paper and have particular times when you look at your bits of paper, and in between times try to forget some of the morass of material. Invest in a diary with plenty of space for each day and write *everything* in it – don't assume that you can hold *anything*, however trivial, in your brain. The only way of being relieved of the pressure of carrying it in your head is to write it down. You have to make it part of your morning routine to look in the diary too. Look at today and the next couple of days, and get the shape of this day and the next two clear in your mind.

A set of spiral notebooks may help you, too. I have three: one for short-term plans, one for long-term plans, and one for bright ideas, because when my brain is really reeling it seems to be material in those three categories hurtling around in it. Writing them down relieves me of the fear that I might forget things that are important and collects all the material together in a useful way. See what the main themes are which buzz around your mind like low-flying aircraft, and find safe homes for them in notebooks.

Changing rôle, environment and emphasis during the day may present you and your children with difficult transitional periods. Some women with dual careers prefer to compartmentalize work and home as completely separate from one another. They wear particular clothes for work and change as soon as they get home, do not think or talk about work at home or home at work, and have a completely different persona in the two different contexts. Others feel it's important to 'be themselves' in both places, and try to build bridges between the two worlds or merge them. Most of us flounder a bit between these two attitudes. All of us have to make a changeover twice a day at least. It would be nice to start the day with coffee, toast, a little light conversation about your plans, and an affectionate goodbye. It would be *lovely* to walk in in the evening tired but satisfied, to the embrace of your excited children, and settle down in a cosy armchair for a cuddle and chat. More often, though, the day starts with a wrangle about lunchboxes, lost car keys, indelible spills down clean shirt fronts: and ends with a rush to pour a large gin and defrost an indescribable lump of frozen food.

One way of tackling the morning and evening changeover is to find a ritual, any ritual to carry you through. In the mornings, unfortunately, organization is probably the key. A haphazard rush may have some feeling of fun when it's just you, but has few charms when shared with four or five other angry, tired people. If you keep losing the car keys, put a hook up and make sure you always hang them there. Organize packed lunches the night before, and make family members responsible for their own packed lunches the *minute* they're old enough. Pack your briefcase and organize your paperwork or whatever the tools of your trade are, in the evening for the following day, or set the alarm ten minutes earlier so you actually allow the time you need for this job. Evolve some sort of pattern for who does what to prepare and clear up breakfast, so it happens reasonably smoothly however tired you are. In our house, whatever state we're in, however rotten the mood we're all in, in the morning we have an agreement to say a fairly pleasant goodbye to each other – this seems to be useful as otherwise a feeling of disturbance and hurt can persist and distract you during the day. On the few days where this hasn't been possible we have actually all been prepared to go late to work and stay at home until we could make enough peace to say a decent goodbye. This might not be important to everybody, but if it is important to you, work it out and agree it with the members of your household.

At the end of the working day, it may help to get your children into the bath as soon as you come home, however odd a time it may seem to do that; a play in warm water can be very soothing for young children. When you come in leave the post and the telephone messages alone, and sit down to read a story together or watch a TV programme together, just to get used to all being in the same space again. Try not to scurry around. Later on you need some time for your own personal decompression ritual. A quarter or half an hour to read a paper, watch an idiotic soap opera or have a soak in the bath (if your hot water system is up to all this bathing), can make a good bridge between the day and the evening. You might water the plants or walk the dog or play a game; it doesn't matter what it is, but find a short soothing ritual that lets you move from one part of your day to the next.

If you are worried about work you may find your sleep disturbed, particularly if your children are waking you in the night and anxieties about the following day's assignments come into your mind. The vicious circle begins where you worry about coping tomorrow because you haven't had enough sleep, and the more you worry about it the more wide awake you get. It may help to evolve a routine where you visualize leaving your work and any other worries at the top of the stairs, or some other place well away from your bed and bedroom. This works well after a bit of practice, and worrying thoughts do not get you by the throat at three a.m.

It is also useful not to look at the clock. It doesn't particularly help to know that it's half past four in the morning, and it's sometimes easier to fall back asleep if you can feel it might be nearly morning or only just midnight.

If you find it painful to be absorbed at work and have to uproot to go home, or vice versa, it's an inner flexibility you have to cultivate. Consider any examples or imagery that will help you have a feeling of flowing rather than wrenching from one role to another. Think about learning some of the physical disciplines that help build inner as well as outer mobility, such as dance, yoga, t'ai chi or the Feldenkreis method. Acknowledge both parts of your life and see if you can find ways of moving more comfortably from one to the other.

The 'guilt trap' is mentioned over and over again by dual-career women. There is a risk of feeling guilty at home because you aren't at work and guilty at work because you aren't at home. Society shows deep concern about the effect that 'working mothers' have on their children; an oddly misplaced concern in my view, since the demands made on and attitudes towards 'working fathers' have a huge and often damaging effect on their relationships with their children. Watch out for ascribing all your children's problems to the fact that you are at work, or ascribing all your work problems to the fact you have young children at home.

To alleviate this, look at chapter 7, 'Setting Targets and Setting Limits', and try the 'visioning' exercise to be clear what your choices about balance are. Once you have a clear view of what your chosen balance is, try to let your guilt go. Remind yourself that both working and family life tend to go through cycles of conflict, resolutions and plateaux, followed by more conflicts, and so on, whatever your arrangements are.

Your emotional wellbeing can of course be enhanced by paying some attention to your physical wellbeing. We know how a complicated lifestyle can cause us to accumulate an excess of adrenalin in our systems, and how any exercise at all, from walking to skating, swimming, dancing, running, or martial arts, as long as it's regular and done with proper preparation and equipment, will disperse that adrenalin and restore our mood. You may feel so utterly exhausted that you cannot imagine spending any of your precious free time on anything that costs you any effort. Obviously you must gauge the kind of exercise that's appropriate for the phase of your life that you're in; if, for example, you are having broken nights and commuting long distances, it would be better to choose a programme of stretching and relaxing than of long-distance running, but as long as you choose to exercise at a level that's appropriate, you'll find it energizing, not tiring.

The quality of the food you eat may also affect your moods and emotions. With a little planning it is as easy to eat a diet high in fresh fruits, salads and baked potatoes, whole grains and honey as it is to fill yourself with low-nutrition, convenience foods. Your body will thank you fervently for discarding junk food from your diet, by feeling fresher, cleaner and stronger. Your moods will ricochet around less as well.

If you find yourself echoing one politician's marvellous prevarication, 'I'm moving towards a vegetarian position' (well, a lot of us are these days), do be careful to keep your protein intake adequate for your demanding life or you will quickly become anaemic and poorly. For advice on this, try looking at Leslie Kenton's book *Raw Energy* or the chapter on diet in *The Book of Yoga* by the Sivananda Yoga Group.

Under pressure it is all too easy to grab at drugs to alleviate our tension and blur our anxiety. Wanting to be kind to ourselves we may eat great bars of chocolate, or drink cups and cups of coffee, or knock back glasses of wine or shots of whisky or smoke cigarettes. The impulse to give ourselves some pleasure and reward is absolutely right and reasonable, but some of the ways we do it can cause us problems. 'Fixes' of high energy after a concentrated intake of sugar like sweets and candies, are followed within a couple of hours by corresponding 'lows'. If there are spots in your day where you long for a sugary high, try having some fresh fruit instead of processed sweets. The natural sugars in fruits cause less fluctuation in our moods, and the fruits also contain vitamins, fibre and far fewer calories than sweets.

Try counting how many cups of coffee you drink a day. In office work it is easy to get into the habit of punctuating your work with an hourly cup, and also for making coffee for other people to be the usual way to initiate social contact and have a chat with colleagues. Try alternating coffees with fruits or herbal tea drinks (provide your own teabags), or take a bottle of mineral water in to work with you. If you have drunk a great deal of coffee for many years, wean yourself off it gradually; if you give it up suddenly you may feel rather shaky for a while. Remember too that drinks like colas have caffeine in them and will hype you up just as much as coffee.

In many professions the chief way people have of being nice to each other is to give each other alcoholic drinks, and it is easy to get into a habit of drinking far too much. Wanting to control alcoholic intake may be seen as very uncool, as 'being a misery', and therefore be all the harder to do. However, the latest guidelines suggest that the maximum daily safe intake for a woman of average weight is two units of alcohol, that is two glasses of wine, two small measures of spirit or a pint of beer or lager. To get down to that limit it may be necessary to take quite an assertive line for a while, until friends and colleagues get used to it. If you feel your relationship with alcohol is getting out of hand contact Alcoholics Anonymous, whose number will be in your local telephone book.

Frightening numbers of young women are becoming addicted to cigarettes in their teens – apparently partly at least because they believe that smoking helps them to control their weight. Smoking is poisonous for you and the people around you, and wildly expensive both financially and in terms of your health. Everyone has to find their own way out of it – many health clinics run a 'Smokestop' programme, or you could try hypnotherapy or acupuncture as an aid to giving up. You could try weaning yourself off the drug with nicotine chewing gum, or some event in your life may give you the shove you need to stop. Smoking on and off for years, it was not until someone close to me developed cancer that I finally found the determination to give up.

What we need to find is other ways to have pleasure and a sense of sharing in our lives. It is the companionable sharing of a cigarette after weathering a rough time with a colleague that I miss, just as much as the drug itself. It is for me, and from groups and discussions I know for many other women, a slow process to learn to make occasions for small pleasures and moments of rapport and companionship among friends and colleagues without resorting to drugs which, in the overview, we would rather not use excessively.

In previous generations it seems that perhaps women spoke with members of their extended family, or priests or other respected members of the community when they were unhappy. Now we may feel there is no-one to talk to, and go to our doctor, who may not have had much training in how to help constructively. Because of this mismatch tranquillizers may be prescribed inappropriately. The minor tranquillizers (Valium, Librium and so forth) are useful drugs for short-term use backed up with other help and support, but many women have become involuntarily addicted to them for lack of other support (the addictive quality of this type of drug was much under-estimated until the mid-1980s). For help if this has happened to you, you could contact the Involuntary Addiction Support Group. The most important point seems to be to phase the drug out slowly rather than giving up suddenly, and the exercise takes a great deal of courage. Grania describes giving up Valium after taking it several times a week for more than two years as, 'the hardest thing I've ever done'.

Practical exercises

Here are seven short practical exercises to help you start managing your emotions.

1. Deep abdominal breathing

When our emotions are overwhelming we quickly reflect this in shallow, tight breathing, which only adds to our tension, and the fact that we are taking in less oxygen means we are thinking less clearly. Learn this deep steady breathing, and once it is familiar you can slip into it when you need it like slipping into another gear.

Sit comfortably with your legs crossed. If you are tired support your back, leaning against the wall or against the front of a settee or armchair. Sit tall and lengthen the back of your neck. Imagine the crown of your head lifting towards the ceiling. Rest the back of your left hand on your left knee. Join the thumb and second and third fingers. Rest your right hand on your abdomen below the navel. Let your eyes close. Start to breathe a little more deeply and a little more slowly than usual. Hear the breath as it comes and goes in your throat. When your breathing has settled into a steady rhythm start to breathe in through your nose, and out through your mouth. Don't blow the breath away, just part your lips and let it escape. When your breathing is steady like this, become aware of your hand on your abdomen. Start to imagine the breath is going all the way down to your hand, and let the breath out come all the way back from your hand. As you breathe in, you fill up, and your abdomen swells out a little. As you breathe out you empty, and your abdomen collapses back a little. Carry on in your own rhythm for a few minutes. When you are ready to stop, without disturbing yourself too much take your hand away from your abdomen and rest it on your right knee. Let your breathing return to an everyday level. Turn your eyes down so that you see the floor first, and when you feel like it blink your eyes open and get used to the light. Notice how still and peaceful you have become.

2. Alternate nostril breathing

This form of breathing is a useful help for insomnia and panic. Once again, when you become familiar with it, you can slip into it when you need it.

To practise the breathing sit comfortably cross-legged, and support your spine as in the previous exercise. (If you are unable to sleep, you can do the breathing in bed; there is no need to get up and sit up.)

Rest your left hand on your left knee. Place the middle finger of your right hand between your eyebrows and then up slightly, on your forehead. Check that you can close your right nostril with your thumb and your left nostril with your fourth finger. As you get used to the rhythm practise closing the alternate nostrils up with less and less pressure, eventually doing it as delicately as possible. Then begin:

1. Inhale deeply.

2. Close your right nostril with your thumb and exhale through the left.

3. Inhale through the left.

4. Close the left nostril with your fourth finger. Release the right. Exhale through the right.

5. Inhale through the right.

Repeat 2–5 steadily for a few minutes. Feel the breaths getting deeper and slower. Inhale and exhale at an even rate.

When you are ready to stop, finish a cycle and gently take your hand away from your face. Rest your hand on your right knee. Let your breathing return to any everyday level. Turn your eyes down so that you see the floor first and when you are ready blink your eyes open and slowly get used to the light. Notice the sense of equilibrium that you feel.

3. Deep relaxation

Dynamic exercise promotes our physical strength. In deep relaxation we get in touch with our inner strength.

If you feel like it, put some soothing music on. Lie yourself down on the floor. Shift your hips and shoulder blades around until you are comfortable, and check that your centre line is straight.

Become aware of your feet. Notice how they've carried you around all your life! Breathe in, tighten your feet up; exhaling, let them go, let them relax. Where they contact the floor let them sink into the floor a little more.

Now think about your legs – thighs, knees, and calves. Breathe in, tighten up your legs a bit; as you exhale, let go and let your legs go heavy.

Tighten up your buttock muscles and pull your abdomen in towards your spine. Breathe in, then as you exhale relax your hips. Imagine your lower back spreading out. Imagine the back of your waist expanding.

Breathe in and tighten up your hands and arms; exhaling, let them relax.

Notice how your ribs are moving while you breathe. Take a deep breath in, and fill your lungs up to the collar bones, really expanding the rib cage. Blow the breath out of your mouth with a sigh. After that, let the breath come and go as it wants to; don't interfere with it at all.

See if you can release your throat. While the brain chatters, the throat tightens. If you can relax your throat, you can slow down your mind.

Screw your face up, and then let it go. Let your head feel heavy on the ground. Take yourself in your imagination to a peaceful place and lay yourself down there for a rest.

When you feel ready to, gradually surface and take some deeper, slower breaths. Stretch a bit, yawn a bit, and when you want to, roll over and curl up on your side for a while. When you want to, push your hands into the floor and come up.

4. Building confidence

When you spend a great deal of time alone with a little child, it is easy to begin to lose self-confidence, and find it difficult to relate to other adults. To let your confidence grow again, begin by affirming your good qualities. With a friend you trust, try taking three minutes each and talk about yourself, *saying only positive things*. All of us can easily hold forth for much more than three minutes about our weaknesses! Try instead to focus on your strengths. Although it feels awkward and artificial at first, this is a useful exercise for anyone who feels her self-esteem is slipping a little.

5. Affirmation

If you are sitting nervously waiting for a meeting, an interview, an evaluation, a confrontation or whatever, try writing on a scrap

49

of paper the good qualities you are bringing to the situation. Again, we all find it far easier to think of all the ways in which we may be unequal to the challenge – but it is helpful to practise noticing calmly what you are good at. Susan used to cycle away from her disastrous driving lessons thinking firmly, 'I'm *not* a fool. I can cook Christmas dinner for twelve with all the trimmings. I'm *not* a fool.' Before leading a stormy team briefing, Nuala wrote down, 'honest attention, good preparation, a lot of experience'. She tucked the piece of paper under the corner of the blotter and glanced at it when her confidence wavered. Reminding herself of those good points helped her keep her equilibrium.

6. Enjoyment

When your life becomes an obstacle race of grim endeavour and coping, build some small pleasures into your life. Make a list of, say, 20 things you enjoy, specific, small and manageable: fresh flowers on the desk; writing with an ink pen; wearing some favourite piece of clothing or jewellery; having a chat to a friend; taking your sandwiches to the park; anything at all that gives you a definite sense of pleasure. Jot down next to each item when you last enjoyed this particular pleasure. If it's all weeks or months ago, respond strongly. Plan one good thing to give yourself each day; then make sure you do!

7. Free drawing

Keep in a dark drawer some plain paper and some crayons or felt tips heavily labelled NOT TO BE USED BY CHILDREN. Share them with your children and you'll never see them again, except in the shape of felt tips left unlidded on the settee's loose covers, a huge blot of ink radiating serenely out from the nib! If you feel totally jangled up and confused emotionally, get your paper and colours out and draw. Start by doodling, and make as many pictures as you want, allowing your drawings to gather energy as you go along. We can all draw – as toddlers we all drew unerringly and unhesitatingly. Sadly, most of us decide or get told at some point after the age of eight that we *can't* draw, and we lose this lovely relaxing resource of expression and exploration.

The activity of drawing, once you 'get into' it, is soothing in itself. When you've had enough and feel like stopping, you may want to look at your pictures and see if they have anything to tell you. Don't try to 'analyse' a drawing. Just see if any mood, or pattern, or shape, comes out of it. Keep this exercise in mind for times when you feel churned up and are not sure why.

6

Managing Health

Health is not an exam that we fail if we're ill and pass if we're well. Health is what our bodies do about how we're living. Taking care of health is unfortunately often something we do only after things go wrong – a positive plan for good health would be a new move for many of us. In an intellect-centred culture, the danger is that we use our bodies simply as things to carry our heads around on top of. We would never expect a car, for example, to function for years on end without some maintenance, but we do sometimes expect this of our long-suffering bodies. Furthermore, neglecting our health not only causes problems, it causes us to miss out on the intense pleasure of a well body.

Taking care to have a fresh, varied, light diet, and some kind of regular exercise, we have already emphasized as essential for our wellbeing. Paying good attention to balancing emotional life will also have a positive effect on physical health.

Healthy eating

It is, of course, simplistic to say to most women, 'have a fresh, light, varied diet'. Our struggles with self-image, thinness, and obsession with weight and size frequently make our relationship with food a complicated one. Anorexia, bulimia, and compulsive eating are the more extreme manifestations of a disturbed relationship with food. Less acute but more common is the on–off dieting with which many of us weaken our bodies and confuse our digestive systems and emotions alike. We look with envy at the few women who have a truly relaxed easy-going attitude to food, eating and size.

Well-educated, high-achieving young women are those most vulnerable to eating disorders. Few men succumb to anorexia or bulimia, those that do often being in extremely high stress jobs like the futures market. If you or anybody close to you is suffering from anorexia or bulimia, you must try to respond. These conditions not only cause the sufferer and those around her terrible anguish, they are life-threatening. Unfortunately, they also often occasion denial and shame which make it very hard for the person involved to acknowledge her condition and the danger she is in. Extreme control over food intake seems to be an agonised metaphor for trying to get control of one's life. Anorexia and bulimia can be treated by therapy or counselling – go to your Well Woman Centre or GP in the first instance to find out what is available. (Addresses, Anorexic Aid, Bulimia Support etc.). As always, in acute and sudden crisis, you can call the Samaritans (number in your local telephone book).

To help us in the long term to understand these conditions more clearly, it is useful to read *The Art of Starvation* by Sheila Macleod: she describes vividly her experience of slipping in and out of anorexia during her adolescence and early and middle twenties, and her own insights into enduring and surviving. Kim Chernin's book *The Hungry Self* tells of the women who came to her for therapy while struggling with the bingeing-and-vomiting cycle of bulimia, and how often a hunger for and then a rejection of the food represents a search for a possible self in a morass of domestic emotional blackmail and cultural confusion. These books have a great deal to say to all women, not just those with anorexia or bulimia.

On-and-off dieting leaves your physical system unsure how much nutrition to expect and therefore unsure at what rate to metabolize food. Teeth, bones, hair, skin and muscle tone all suffer in the confusion. Emotionally you put yourself in the position of having days when you're 'good' (as in 'I've been good today, I've only had half a lettuce leaf') and 'bad' ('I was really wicked and ate some chocolate on the bus'). Also one has days where one feels 'fat' and days where one feels 'thin' (sometimes *only* according to what you know you've eaten, with no actual variation in weight or size at all) and a congruent fluctuation in one's sense of one's own ability and worth.

And all this in the context of a world where a third of the population spend all of their energy trying to get enough to eat,

53

and many of them still die of hunger. Any time any woman can ease up her anxiety about food and size, or come to celebrate the enjoyment of food in an easy way, and celebrate her body at its own comfortable size, she helps not only herself but all the other women in her life to undo the cultural grip of these obsessions. If you want to do this but don't know where to start, there is no simple answer – but any way in which you explore and extend your relationship with your own body, and any information and ideas that deepen your awareness of cultural conditioning of body image, will help.

The female body

The lunar rhythm of the menstrual cycle is constantly with us, interrupted by pregnancy, and eventually transformed by the menopause. Popular mythology has it that women are 'always' taking time off for 'women's problems', but in fact women workers take fewer occasional days off work than men, and are generally speaking stoical about the considerable physical challenges of menstruation, pregnancy, birth, lactation and the menopause.

The menstrual cycle

Although every tabloid newspaper exploits the sexuality of women in daily photographs of breasts, no woman is allowed to let her period, just as much a part of her sexuality, become visible in any way at all. Sanitary towels and tampons (still carrying VAT as luxury goods!) must be kept hidden, and stains and marks are absolutely taboo. One of the times in my life when I have felt most embarrassed (as opposed to the many and various times when I've felt foolish) was during a martial arts training session when there were no other women present and I bled slightly but steadily onto my uniform, not realizing until after the class was over. I felt as though I had done something deliberately offensive, and yet since about 25% of the women in the world are presumably bleeding at any one time that feeling is surely inappropriate. Nevertheless it is considered inappropriate in most mixed company even to acknowledge that periods happen, let alone to cope with any actual blood.

Some women change up and down through the monthly hormonal gears happily, without tension or discomfort. However, the rhythm of emotions, variable energy, cramps and release is part of your life, and cannot be denied. It seems better to do what you can to minimize any unpleasantness and try to find a positive sense of the whole cycle. The practice of hatha yoga is particularly good for easing any bloated or tender sensations pre-menstrually and the Lotus Yoga Mudra pose helps to relieve menstrual cramp. Self-administered Shiatsu is reported by many women as helpful in releasing pre-menstrual emotional tension. Marking the days of the period itself in some positive way may help. Alison says she took her cue from the *Dame aux Cammelias* (who wore pink camellias during her period) and decided to find some particular piece of jewellery to wear on those days. Eventually she chose some earrings in the shape of crescent moons. John and Farida Davidson, in their book *Natural Fertility Awareness*, make the point that so many women spend so many years on the Pill, where their cycle is suppressed, that they find the rhythm shocking and intense when they do come back to it, not having the lifetime of practice that women of previous generations did. It seems important not to evade or divert all sorts of other worries into the category of 'pre-menstrual tension', thereby feeding the myth that women's bodies are temperamental and malign, but rather to find ways of harmonizing with the ebb and flow of the cycle.

Pregnancy

The cycle itself changes with pregnancy and with the menopause. Managing pregnancy among colleagues as well as in one's personal life may take some considerable effort. Notify your personnel officer as soon as you reach 12 weeks to discuss details of maternity leave and maternity pay, and also pencil in the date on which you have to decide whether you will be taking up your job again, and the date on which you will have to notify your employer of your return.

Enough rest and good nutrition are absolutely essential if you are to continue working throughout your pregnancy; alter your régime if you have to to ensure these. Work away from VDUs, as much as you can (consult your firm's Occupational Health Officer, or ring your local Health and Safety Department for up-to-date information on the minimum safety standards for pregnant women near VDUs). Do the 'ten minute pick-me-up' on page 56 of *Exercises for Childbirth* by Barbara Dale and Johanna Roeber, in your lunch break.

Emotionally you need to be very flexible, both within yourself and in dealing with colleagues. You may feel pressurized and tense about having to prove you can still do your job, and you may feel anxious about asserting that you plan to keep your job after your child is born. In yourself you need a gentle observant ability to adapt, and with others, a light assertiveness. If possible you need a friend and confidante who is also pregnant and working, but not in the same place as you.

It is no good making a rigid decision inside yourself about how long you intend to work and when and how you intend to return, even if you have to make an appearance of doing so. Each phase of the pregnancy has its own character and it seems more positive to respond to it as you go along. The choice is not a rigid one between being Superwoman in a tailored suit and Earthmother in a flowered smock; you don't have to be *either* at the Fax machine *or* making homemade bread. You can try to evolve your own identity as you go along – it's hard and exhausting, but much more creative and rewarding in the end.

You may find yourself unexpectedly introspective from the fourth month on, involved in an inner dialogue with the little being kicking inside you. You may find yourself gazing out of the window with unprecedented spiritual intimations floating through your mind, and will almost certainly find yourself more upset and deeply affected by distressing news items than in other parts of your life. Obviously you can't spend hours at work meditating on your baby, and cogitating on the meaning of Life, the Universe and Everything; but you can keep a part of yourself in touch with the baby all the time, and you can make space in your own time for whatever the quiet part of you marvelling at the miracle of the child needs – walks in the country, listening to peaceful music, whatever you feel you want.

Many women report a definite disengaging from intellectual activity from the thirty-fourth week or so, so it would be better to make sure that you have nothing too intellectually demanding to cope with from roughly then on. Even postgraduates in astrophysics seem to find that magazine problem pages are the maximum level of reading they can be bothered with by week thirty-four, and this reluctance to extend much attention beyond your body, your baby and yourself seem quite appropriate as you gather your resources together inside yourself ready for the birth.

Colleagues may make devastating or insulting comments, presumably not realizing how rude they're being. One woman who loved her job as an administrator in a busy airport was told by a male colleague: '*You* won't be back – you're much too *nice* to leave your baby.' Julia, who went back to work in a multinational corporation part time after her son was born, was constantly treated to snide remarks about, 'Oh God, here comes the part timer again', although, as she says, they are getting very good value for money since she *thinks* about the job far more than part time, and often comes up with ideas and solutions while turning work over in her mind at home. Jane's boss on a scientific research project acknowledged this when he told her: 'In you we get a full-time brain for a part-time salary', but when she became pregnant with her second child devastated her by announcing that, 'part timers aren't committed', and citing her second pregnancy as proof that she personally was not committed to science. A general undercurrent of knowing and sarcastic ridicule may bother you: 'Oh, you *think* you'll manage, but that's what they all say, you'll find you don't want to carry on when it comes to the crunch.' 'Carrying on working? Oh, yes. I've heard that one before!' Protect yourself from feeling too hurt by this kind of thing. It comes partly from jealousy (I think everyone, men and women, have at least a flicker of jealousy towards a woman walking around carrying the wonder of another human being inside her), and partly because it challenges everyone's compartmentalized views about work, home and a woman's place. In my view it has little to do with the pregnant woman's or new mother's impaired output. If you analysed which was greater, output compromised by pregnancy or motherhood, as against, say, output compromised by social drinking of alcohol, in most organizations, I know which my money would be on.

Don't let other people's confusion and thoughtless remarks push you into a rigid stance. Do what feels right for you. Practise meeting idiotic comments assertively, with phrases such as, 'I feel you're being unhelpful/patronizing here', or, 'I feel upset and angry about the things you're saying.'

The menopause

The fertile part of our life finally changes with the menopause which may happen at as early an age as 38 or as late as the late 50s. You may be aghast to find your children entering the turbulence of adolescence just as you hit the stormy waters of the menopause. Getting sensible and non-sexist help and advice seems to depend on the networking of women rather than official channels. There is a helpful chapter on the menopause in Sheila Kitzinger's excellent *Woman's Experience of Sex*, and Well Woman Centres run workshops and discussion groups on the subject.

Marie, at work part time and bringing up three teenage children single-handed, describes the main issues for her:

I was increasingly vulnerable emotionally and experienced hot flushes day and night which I found very difficult. I also on a couple of occasions was shocked to have sudden haemorrhages without any warning cramps, once in an exercise class and once in a supermarket queue. The class was all women so that was OK, I didn't feel too bad, but when it happened in the shop I just left my shopping and ran. Thank God it never happened at work.

I also felt grief at knowing I was no longer fruitful. I certainly didn't want more children but I was sad to let the capacity to have a baby go.

Marie developed a many-layered style of clothing to cope unobtrusively with sudden swoops and dips in her body temperature. Emotionally she relied on her good friendships with other women to try to find a perspective on things. The sudden bleeds were hard to cope with, since they were so unpredictable. Carrying tampons and sanitary towels everywhere was obviously sensible, but wearing panty liners all the time just in case was expensive and uncomfortable.

Her feeling is that the menopause is treated culturally as a sort of horrible undignified joke, like mothers-in-law, and that she is having to work out, very much alone and pioneering, a good and positive way to get through the menopause. Even for those of us who assume our menopause will be quite a way into the future, it may be useful to start acknowledging it as a part of one's life as a woman and to think over possible approaches and attitudes to this part of our physical rhythm.

Disease and illness

Disease: if we separate the parts of the word we find dis-ease; the body out of key, out of gear, out of joint, jangled up, and perhaps invaded by bacteria or virus. Women, like everybody else, are vulnerable to big scarey diseases and small inconvenient ones. Positive health should be our aim, but we need information about dis-ease too. A good basic resource is a copy of *Our Bodies Ourselves* by the Boston Women's Health Collective, which explains a great deal about both health and illness.

Of the big scarey illnesses, the two that probably stand out in most of our minds are cancer and AIDS. Both cervical smears and breast scans are available on the National Health at your GP or at the Family Planning Clinic. Some firms and organizations also organize scanning and smears for female staff. Although some women find the smear test uncomfortable and the breast scan embarrassing, we should always take the opportunity to have these observations done, since these are cancers that have a very good chance of cure if they are noticed early enough.

The AIDS virus has come to our notice in the middle of the 1980s as something of which we all need to be aware. Anyone can catch AIDS who takes part in at-risk activities: that is, penetrative sexual intercourse with an infected person, or sharing a hypodermic needle with an infected person to inject drugs. Although some research is going into drugs to relieve or cure AIDS, the virus itself is mutating so fast that it seems rash to rely on a cure being found in the foreseeable future. Our priority for ourselves, our partners, our friends and our children must be prevention.

If you do inject drugs, firstly never, never share a needle, and secondly, consider seeking counselling and support to help you deal with your life without the drugs which will, without a doubt, wreck your body in the end.

If you have penetrative sexual intercourse with anyone other than an exclusive partner, use a condom. If you are in a part of your life where you do sleep with different people at different times, carry condoms yourself so you've always got one if you need one. Carrying condoms in the late twentieth century implies responsibility, not promiscuity.

In a discussion about AIDS the point was made that you are safe if you are in an exclusive pair-bond relationship. 'Well,' said Sarah laconically, 'of course, that's what we all *hope* we've got.' A silence fell. The need for trust and integrity in sexual partnerships has never been so great.

Randy Shilt's long but fascinating book *And The Band Played On* chronicles the way AIDS arose, the reactions of politicians, of the medical community, the homosexual community, and the growth and changes people have gone through because of the epidemic. For confidential information and advice about AIDS, ring Frontliners.

AIDS and blood have become inextricably linked in our minds, and rightly so, but it is quite impossible to catch AIDS by *giving* blood. Blood stocks have become very low because our unconscious association between blood and AIDS has led to a reluctance to give blood, but the Blood Donation Service ask us to disentangle our thoughts on the subject and give blood as and when we can. Any of us or our loved ones might need blood in an emergency and we would hate to think of there not being enough for them, so we should donate when we can.

Small inconvenient illnesses mostly indicate that one is run down. Cultivate the art of taking the odd day off sick if you need to, rather than soldiering on and needing a week off for a major bout of flu or whatever in the end. Get to know your body so that you can recognize whether what ails you is sadness or a temperature, lassitude or flu. Plan your work so that you can delegate for a day or two occasionally if necessary. We are all dispensable – when we do take to our beds, surprising though it is, the Universe continues to function.

If you need to call a doctor, use your assertiveness to communicate and ask questions. Doctors have little training in communicating in any other than an authoritarian or patronizing way: it takes a very exceptional person to get through medical training and the stressful early years of practice without picking these mannerisms up. Nevertheless, it is your body, and you have a right to ask what you need to know about it. Ask for clear information about any drugs you may need to use. Marge Piercey's insight leapt out from her book *A Woman on the Edge of Time* with a blinding flash to me. 'There are no side effects to drugs,' she says 'only effects.' True.

If you need an appointment at the surgery, try to get the first appointment in the morning. At our surgery even that one can be 35 minutes late, but at least the delay doesn't run into hours. If you have to take a later appointment, take a pleasant book, do some deep breathing, and be philosophical – keep your blood pressure low! Block bookings on hospital antenatal clinics are notorious, delays chronic. Take *War and Peace* (or similar) with you. If you have the energy, write to the chief administrator of your hospital with copies to the chief obstetrician, asking why they continue to make appointments in this way that is profoundly disrespectful to pregnant women.

You may also find you take much of the responsibility for your children's health, and perhaps also your partner's. Your children *will* sometimes be ill, so you must make contingency plans (see chapter 2). Negotiate with your nanny or childminder as to whether she will take them for routine appointments such as inoculations or dentist's, and decide whether you want to be there if something painful like an injection is going to happen.

Finally, being healthy is a complex and creative enterprise. Our best chance for finding health in a polluted and tense environment seems to be to avoid health fetishes and take a broad, moderate, and holistic approach to keeping well.

7

Setting Targets and
Setting Limits

Feeling that to do otherwise would sound unpleasantly grasping, some of the most successful women I know still describe their careers as though they were accidental. For instance, the editor of a newspaper woman's page said, 'I'm only here because of a series of cock-ups.' Possibly – but it seems very unlikely. Luck does of course have a part to play in how our careers develop, but so does conscious planning. Careful and flexible planning, including considered decisions about parameters and limits, may help you to steer your working life in the way you want, leaving you with less of a sense of being the by-product of a 'series of cock-ups'.

Begin by taking a look at your future and your hopes for that future. Two things need clearing out of the way. One is, 'I'll do it when . . .' and the other is timidity of vision. 'I'll get on with that when I've done the ironing, when the children are at school, when the weather's better, when Christmas is over . . .' and so on. Our habit tends to be to be reactive, to wait until something else is sorted out. It is how our lives as women tend to go. As Ann Oakley observed, women are always waiting – waiting to be asked to dance, waiting to be asked to get married, waiting till someone gets home, waiting at the doctor's surgery, waiting in the playground, waiting at the checkout. No wonder women get so much less agitated than men in traffic jams; they have so much more practice at waiting patiently. A group of professional women compiled a list of things they're 'waiting for', as part of an exercise. Their list included:

I'm waiting till I'm 7½ stone
   till I've had my period
   till after the holidays
   till the children grow up

till I get my exam results
till I move house
till my husband's less worried about *his* job.

Make a list of the things *you* tend to wait for. Some may be unavoidable hold-ups, but mark with an asterisk any that you would like to stop procrastinating for.

Thinking about unlimited vision, it is hard at first to believe how much you *may* achieve. A lifetime's messages about your limitations or lack of ability may be holding you up. Throw modesty to the winds and try out, as you might try on different clothes, the thought of yourself in various different jobs, at various different levels. Be like the Red Queen in *Alice Through the Looking Glass*: 'Why, sometimes I've believed as many as six impossible things before breakfast.' (Though, of course, these things only *feel* impossible. They may be perfectly feasible.) Try out your daring in this visionary exercise (if possible do this in the company of a friend in a similar situation):

1. Make a list of all the things you want to do in your life, ever. Take your time. Include learning languages, passing exams, achieving exercise targets, getting promotions, how much you want to earn, places you want to travel to, things you want to happen within your family life. Include anything else you want to do.

2. From your first list, abstract a list of things you'd like to do in the next five years.

3. From your second list, abstract a list of the things you'd like to do in the next 12 months.

4. Write an affirmative paragraph describing yourself doing and achieving all the things you would like to manage in the next 12 months. (If you are doing this work with a friend, share your paragraphs with each other.)

5. Make an action plan, concentrating on the action you need to take to achieve the goals you want to in the next year, but including references to the five-year and rest-of-your life lists if appropriate. Remember the acronym SMART (see p. 24) for

action planning: Specific, Manageable, Achievable, Realistic, and Time Targeted.

6. Make notes on the 'force field' around your action planning. What factors are helping you to make the changes or moves you need to make? What factors are stopping you or making it difficult for you to take action? Look first at the 'anti' forces that seem to be stopping you. Try to decide which are just excuses for not getting to grips with things, and which are genuinely holding you up – and look at ways to minimize these. Next look at the 'pro' forces that are helpful to you in your efforts, and notice any ways that you can boost these even more. If you are doing this exercise with a friend who is in the same boat, her feedback and discussion will be useful to you here.

7. If you have worked through this material with a friend, make a commitment to review it again in three to six months to see how you are both getting on, and to see whether you need to adapt your plan and if so how. Your mutual support and involvement in each other's progress will be useful.

This 'visioning' exercise has a holistic feel to it and looks at your life in the round. You may want to take an approach more focused on your current working situation.

Call to mind all the things that are going on for you at work at this moment, then make three lists:

- problems to solve
- initiatives to take
- promotion or training to aim for

Highlight the two or three items on each list that seem to be most important and set yourself some targets on each of them, remembering to identify the time by which you want to have started your action.

Clearly, you change, and the circumstances at your work change, and it might be useful to pencil into your diary a date roughly every three months where you look at your situation and clarify your thoughts on those three headings: problems to solve, initiatives to take and promotion or training to aim for.

You may be able to crystallize what your aims are from those two exercises. If you can't because you don't have a clear sense of how you want to proceed, try one of the next two, which may help you to sort out what you do want to set as your targets.

Drawing your life line

Take a large piece of paper and on it draw a line, like a graph, representing your life. Show the high points and the low points: mark in the major events. Look at the pattern you see and notice what the qualities of the high points are. Particularly notice any high points relating to your work. Work on by yourself or discuss with a friend in a similar situation by what sort of changes or progress you want to make to develop those high points or similar high points at work.

This helps to locate what does give you the greatest satisfaction at work, and think about how to increase and extend it.

Enjoyment exercise

Note down 20 activities that you enjoy; off the top of your head, without thinking too hard.

Now look at your list: mark everything that costs more than £10 with a pound sign; mark anything that takes longer than an hour with an asterisk. Put a ring round any of the activities that you haven't done for a year, and underline any that you haven't done for a month.

Then reflect on what you've found out – and take particular notice of any aspects of your work that appear on the list. Again, this may help you to work out where and what to develop. If many items are ringed or underlined, think hard about your life and why you are getting so little enjoyment at the moment. With both this and the 'life line' exercise you need not necessarily come to any immediate conclusions, but let the material you've come up with hang around in your mind for a few days while you think it over.

Networking

Networking is another important resource for women at work trying to work out what their goals and possibilities are. Some women have tried to find for themselves a different model of behaviour from the traditional rat race approach. It may be difficult to maintain, but it seems to be a worthwhile effort, and a chance to make a profound difference to corporate ethics and organizational behaviour. It may be possible for the women you work with and you to give each other help and support. You may even want to get a formal or informal women's group together at work. Sharing experiences, information and leads in a positive and cooperative way with female colleagues, rather than seeing them all as competition, may be a useful way to develop your information, connections and outlook.

A word of warning – it has shocked me repeatedly to see how angry male colleages sometimes become with women who want to do something as innocuous as have lunch together once a month. The reaction of a normally mild-mannered male archaeologist when the women working on site with him were thinking of having an informal confidence-building group once a week had to be seen to be believed. Really it was nothing short of a tantrum, and he had not heard one word of the reasons why they wanted to get together. In fact their sense was that while many women graduate in archaeology, few get to the top of the profession. Ten years after graduation they were depressed to find male colleagues in print and on TV, and they themselves still sitting at the bottom of wet trenches. They felt pretty sure that this was because of their lack of assertiveness rather than lack of ability. However, his performance shocked and frightened them, and on that occasion at least they did not feel able to go ahead with their group.

Angry reactions from men are often a disguised jealousy, or sometimes a sense inside themselves that things really *are* unfair towards women, and therefore a lurking and repressed guilt. Consult Ann Dickson's indispensible book on assertiveness, *A Woman In Your Own Right*, to find ways of avoiding getting 'hooked' into irrelevant arguments about your women's group.

Not all women at work feel able to support and aid women. It is depressing that almost everyone I interviewed for this book, both male and female, spoke of at least one woman of their acquaintance who had a successful career herself, but had 'pulled the ladder up after her'; whose identity, in other words, depends on being an exceptional superwoman who has made it, and is superior to and has little respect for lesser sisters.

Obviously everyone has to decide for herself how to behave in this respect, but my feeling is that future growing success for women in managing our two careers depends on good strong alliances, and in enabling, encouraging and making things easier for each other. This does not mean accepting or encouraging shoddy work, or indulging ourselves or others in unrealistic fantasies, but it does mean developing a 'mind set' or habit of sharing skills, ideas, and progress, rather than hoarding those things in a competitive spirit.

An indirect form of networking is through our relationships with women of the past. The expansion of women's publishers has made available letters, journals, diaries, and autobiographies of women ordinary and extraordinary, in war and in peace, all over the world, rich and poor. Great strength comes from hearing 'herstory' as written by the women themselves, and it's encouraging to find out about the strength, ingenuity, humour, and perceptions of our foremothers.

Finding our own limits

After setting targets, we need to look at the other parameters and set limits. 'I never set limits before, I just ploughed along until I fell flat on my face, and then said "Oh, I seem to have reached a limit here" '; Alana, running her own business, and mother of a 15-month-old son, speaks here. Again, you could try to be more pro-active by mapping out your limits before you fall over them.

Make a list of the pressurizing components of your work. They might include:

physical exhaustion
working in the evenings
anxiety over innovative projects
boredom
commuting
nights away from home
personal conflict
anxiety over clients

Now look at each item and consider how you might like to set some limits. There is obviously a trade-off here, and some items may have to be negotiated with your employers. There may be an effect on your profile and prospects within your organization, but that may be preferable to unbearable stress or conflict. Work out how many nights a month you *are* prepared to be away and how many nights altogether each time. Think about the physical efforts involved in your work and decide what limits you want to impose on those. How many evenings a week are you prepared to work? See if you can make an assessment and a decision. What offers would you move heaven and earth and change all your limits for?

Setting limits has to do with accepting that your energy may be tremendous but it is finite, and with taking responsibility for where your energy is going. It's important to remember how much your life will change over the next ten or fifteen years. You might like to visualize a sliding scale where you have say 60% of your attention with your child or children and 40% with your job in the early years of their lives, gradually moving towards different balances as their stages and needs, and your own, alter. (The proportions would, of course, be quite variable from woman to woman.)

Once you have a child you can never give your whole self to your job again, says everybody, especially people with ambivalent feelings about women attempting to combine the two rôles.

68

Perhaps; but how many people, male or female, who are footloose and fancy free, are actually 'giving everything' to their work? How much energy are they putting into nightlife and finding a partner, or into playing potential employers off against one another, rather than committing themselves to the work in hand? Furthermore, the humanizing and maturing effects of parenthood can only enhance most people's performance in most jobs.

If certain professions (for instance gynaecology and obstetrics, as described by Wendy Savage and others) organize their training programmes so as to almost entirely exclude women, or certain large organizations do the same, a long slow process of change must and will eventually redress the balance. A new emphasis in forward-looking companies on holistic management will, one hopes, eventually bring about the redesign of training programmes and career pathways. Men have nothing to fear from changes that will give them more recognition as human beings, when women who are mothers are seen as valuable and productive individuals just as men who are fathers are.

8

Managing Three Careers

Jane heard that I was working on a book called *Managing Two Careers*. Her comment was: 'I hope somebody's going to write a book soon called *Managing Three Careers*, because that's what I need: I'm dealing with my children, my career, and my husband's career as well.' Her words struck a chord with me and many other women who not only care about their own professional life as well as their family, but also live with a partner who does a demanding job.

When both partners in a family with children have jobs that they are committed to, you really are in the realms of three-dimensional chess as you try to sort your priorities out. Fairness, realism, clear thinking, good negotiating skills, determination and kindness are all essential. Clairvoyance would be an advantage, but is not normally available so decisions have to be made without benefit of foreknowledge.

When two careers are running in a partnership, issues arise whether you both enter the third career of parenthood or not. One is a competitive element. If you both passed similar exams and entered similar professions, you may be acutely aware of which of you is 'getting on' more quickly, and who is earning the most. If the partnership lasts over several years there will probably be ebbs and flows on both sides: times when one of you is ahead, and times when the other one is. There will probably also be some times when one of you feels more satisfied and fulfilled at work than the other. If you are in a less fulfilling phase yourself it is hard not to feel jealous when your partner is in a radiant state of satisfaction, or very preoccupied and absorbed with the details of his work. Two things may help: one is to try to take the long view, and understand that the ups and downs often level out. The other is not to bottle the feeling up, not to be afraid to admit to these rather inelegant emotions, and to try to discuss them in a constructive way. If your career waxes while your partner's wanes, of course, you should try to be considerate about their feeling of anxiety and vulnerability about being 'left behind'.

While your children are young it is likely that your working life will be moving at a different rhythm and pace from that of your partner's, and perhaps a slower one, unless you are one of the few partnerships where the man is undertaking all or most of the childcare or child management (and even then, the most egalitarian of men cannot undertake pregnancy and birth). (Incidentally, for pompous men who claim 'I'm more of a feminist than my wife', I recommend the question 'who cleans out the toilet in your house?') To deal with any rising panic or sense of being 'left behind', it may be a good time to make some really long-term plans, looking five or ten years ahead, and sketching in the basic shape of your working life well ahead, so that you do not feel as though you have lost all momentum. Your sketch is, of course, only a 'working drawing', and can be changed and adapted at any time; what it shows is your belief in the professional side of yourself at a time when that part of your self-image feels a bit shaky.

If you have already 'made your mark' at work, you may find a slowing of pace while your children are young is actually a wonderful chance for reappraisal. Genevieve, a senior personnel officer at a major retail chain, had her first baby in her early thirties. Having been a high flyer she no longer felt any need to prove herself to herself or anybody else in professional terms. She described the deep tiredness she felt after years of taking care of other people's problems in her personnel work, and how she was gradually letting that tiredness seep out. She felt delight in seeing her horizons broadening – thinking about the many directions her work career could now take and using the time while her child is young to take a good look around. For her the 'slowing-down' is a positive opportunity rather than a difficulty to be minimized.

On top of unsynchronized waves of success or failure, you have to grapple with geography. There comes a tide in the affairs of many junior executives where they 'have' to move areas in order to progress up the hierarchy. This tide often comes at roughly the time their children are babies. What this means in human terms is uprooting the family and placing them in a new environment at a time when they all feel pretty vulnerable, and placing the woman (if she is *not* the executive in this case) in a new place away from all her old connections and associates just when she needs all the network and support she can get, to work out how to manage her two (or three) careers. Small wonder many women give up at this point. Owing to the vagaries of the English house-buying system, the longeurs of solicitors and so forth, families are often separated for months at this point, while one partner sells the old house and the other copes in the new place with a scary new job and no proper place to live. During one of my broke periods I worked in a wine bar, and often met miserable, lonely men who had moved on ahead of their families to start the next phase of their career, separated from loving support exactly when they needed it most. I used to think too of their partners and children, equally lonely and fed up, and unlike the men, not able to get out for a drink to cheer themselves up.

If the big corporations worked out properly what unhappiness, marital breakdown, and loneliness, cost in financial terms to them (let alone any other criteria) they would surely take more care in timing and expediting relocation of staff.

Depending on your partnership and on how confident or otherwise your partner feels about negotiating change with his employers, you may be able at least to time your relocations and perhaps think about your priorities.

If you find yourself in a new and unfamiliar place with two bewildered toddlers, a tense husband and a house that needs (say) rewiring, you are going to have to be ingenious and determined, and decide to swim and not sink. If you can, form an alliance with at least one other person in the new environment similarly placed. If you can't find anyone in the new place take time to stay in touch with someone from the old place with whom you don't have to pretend. Two people raging together about feelings of powerlessness soon work out ways of becoming more powerful (but make sure you rage and don't wallow).

Sasha talks about her first weeks in a new house when her husband's firm moved him on:

When we came here Josh was two and baby Mark was five months old. We lived on a new estate in a tide of mud where the building wasn't all finished. It was a 'dormitory' estate – the men all left for work in the mornings and these sort of dolls' houses all echoed with silence. I was shocked how much I missed my old friends and how Josh really mourned his friends from where we used to live. I could not believe that five years ago I had been at college, free to live my own life, busy and popular, and that three years ago I had been a working girl with my own money, going out for dinner, having fun, and that now I was stuck in this place where I knew no-one, exhausted by broken nights and endless repetitive jobs. I nearly despaired at that point. Then, I decided it was just not going to get the better of me, I was going to make it work out. I love flowers, but we didn't have any, we hadn't made a garden at that stage; but I used to put a jamjar with dandelions in it on the table, fresh each day, and that was my promise to myself that I was going to survive and make a life here.

Start finding a network however you can (clubs and societies, church, sports, community centre, library notice board, adult education classes, anything that gets you out and doing something specific as an individual at least once a week) and build on from there. When faced with emotional wrenches and logistical problems simultaneously in family life, I have sometimes used the mental trick of pretending it was an artificial management problem set on a training course. This somehow gives me an emotional distance, prevents me from getting paralysed by panic, and gives me more access to my intellect for looking for intelligent ways to 'problem-solve'.

What happens if an opportunity comes up for you where you would need to move, what would happen? Would the family move for the sake of your career? Maybe, and maybe not. Beverly says that her family *has* moved for her job, and *not* moved for her partner's job. Her conclusion is this:

I think perhaps you have to decide which person is going to have the career with most clout. In our household it's mine. I'm just far more ambitious – my ambition thermostat is set higher than his if you like. It works out fine.

In chapter 1 Jane described how she evolved or invented for herself a new career in science after the birth of her second baby. Here she discussed how she and her husband, who is a policeman moving swiftly up through the ranks, co-ordinate their lives:

John's job demands 100% commitment to the community he's policing and to the 120 men and women under his command. He deals with their operational needs and personal needs – he might have to be in a counselling rôle if a member of staff has, say, marital or drink problems, or a WPC is finding it hard to deal with teasing from the men. Because he's expected to do well he's consulted on all kinds of other projects. In public order situations he's the one who has to decide when to open another box of policemen, when to pull people out if they're tired – all that. He doesn't work shifts as such but has to stay on if there is a crisis – and he does sometimes do a night shift and have late meetings.

This all adds up to the sort of career with which many women would feel most inhibited about trying to coordinate their own. It's worthy, exhausting, involves irregular hours and demands tremendous support from 'the wife'. However, both John and Jane are dedicated to their work and respect each other's dedication. The love between the two of them, and them and their children, is manifest. Jane describes how they have begun to work things out. She explains how they got together in the first place:

We met at University at the Freshers' Dance. I spent months trying to convince myself I didn't really like him because it seemed such a cliché – but I couldn't. We always thought our partnership would be fair and equal. He started off as a drama teacher but disliked it, changed direction, and was accepted into the police force. He made the first sacrifice and we moved for *my* first job – but I made the next one because I was offered a job in Dundee which would have made life difficult for him because Scottish law is very different. I didn't take the post.

However, we both got posts in Nottingham; he was moving up fast. At every stage he enjoyed the work and found he could do it well. The joy for him is 'being there'. He loves to be there when things happen and to be in touch with people's lives.

At this point Jane pulled out a paperback copy of Joseph Wambaugh's book *The Onion Field*, and showed this paragraph about policework, clearly still moved by what moves John:

He felt that the job was not particularly hazardous physically but was incredibly hazardous emotionally and too often led to divorce, alcoholism and suicide. No, policemen were not danger lovers, they were seekers of the awesome, the incredible even the unspeakable in human experience. To be there *was the thing.*

However, this diplomatic alternating of 'sacrifices' could not continue. Jane continues:

The crunch came when he was offered a place on a course that would lead to a big promotion. I was pregnant with our second child and feeling vulnerable. The course was four months away from home – September to December inclusive. Our baby was due the following February. What shattered me was that there was no question in his mind about whether he should go or not. He didn't come home and discuss it, he came home and told me he was going – how could I say 'no' or have any doubt. It was such an opportunity.

Well, that evening we had hours of very intense discussion. We tried to go to bed at midnight but couldn't sleep so we got up again and talked till three a.m. In the end he saw why I was so hurt. If he went away it would be really hard for me to keep my work up as well as look after our daughter and run everything single-handed and cope with advanced pregnancy. I said 'How would you feel if somebody said to you "from tomorrow you won't be a policeman any more"; because I feel as though the consequence of you going away is that you or the world is saying to me "from tomorrow you won't be a scientist any more". Then he understood.

He went, but he went realizing what he was doing. I held out at work. What suffered was I felt I wasn't giving our daughter as nice a life as I wanted to give her, and I didn't have time to pay attention to my pregnancy – I couldn't as it were reflect on the baby properly.

It's exciting now because I'm actually managing my own career, which I wasn't before, and I've got a good balance, and John and I can work it out. If your partner has a rigid and inflexible job something's got to give. It's been a hard lesson for me to learn because when I left university it never occurred to me it was going to be as difficult as this.

John insists that he too is managing three careers and that in doing so he too is breaking new ground, particularly in an organization like the police force. He says:

When we were expecting a baby, I always felt *we* were expecting a baby. I'm surprised when my staff come in to see me and say *'my wife's* expecting a baby'; to me it was a shared thing we were doing together. One of my men also said recently 'I cannot get used to the sight of my Super, pushing a pushchair in the mornings'; he sees me taking our daughter to playschool.

I asked Jane if there is an excitement in science for her similar to John's excitement about 'being there'. She replied:

I want to know why things are as they are. It's the same thing really. He's interested in societal terms, and I'm interested in physical terms – what the molecules are doing. It's the fact that we have that in common helps us to understand what each other is trying to do and why.'

She concludes by saying:

If I give up now, it will be more difficult for my daughter when she grows up to integrate work and motherhood. I'm a sort of foot soldier, finding out the territory.

9

Managing Love

Of all the headings in this book, love is probably the least manageable in a pro-active intellectual sense. Love comes and goes, takes us by surprise, fills us with delight, or leaves us devastated, in a way that perhaps more than with any of our other 'subjects' is out of our control.

If you live with a partner, the love you share with him or her probably feels like the most important loving in your life. The police force, the civil service, the teaching profession and many others had a marriage bar for women well into this century. Women have fought and fought hard to be allowed both marriage or partnership, a family and a career. Now we have the task of trying to make it all work. You may have held your head high and hammered out an equal relationship with your partner that facilitated an equal emotional relationship, only to find that the increased vulnerability of pregnancy changed your equilibrium and made you want a different kind of love, or that the weeks at home on maternity leave created a different deployment of chores, and the broken nights and physiology of breastfeeding changed your sense of what you as a person need in terms of support, affection and an outside job. The intensity of love, the quality of love, that we want to give and receive may change many times during the years around childbearing.

If you both work outside the home it's important to think hard about good time management in order to get some time together, to keep that thread of loving partnership running through your life. Couples vary as to how much time they want and need to keep their relationship alive and loving. Don't let your time together get diminished and eroded until it vanishes. Work out how much time you want and need and defend it! Jenny explains:

We find we need half an hour to ourselves when Adrian comes home, to make contact again, and just quickly catch up on what we've both done during the day. Then during the evening we've both got a lot to do, we share getting the children bathed and into bed and washing up, and then we both get on with our own things. After that at about ten o'clock we sit and talk and have a cup of tea for about an hour, a more relaxed chat before we go to bed.

Those two bits of time seem to work for them in keeping them in touch and feeling close. However, when asked if this was easy or difficult she laughed and said:

Difficult, very difficult. All our children (two girls of school age and a baby boy) try to sabotage the early evening time by barging in and out, and even by physically pushing us apart, by demanding food and drinks, falling over accidentally-on-purpose – they are very jealous when we talk to one another. In our late evening time the baby sometimes wakes up too. We hang on to those times though – we've seen too many friends drift apart because they gradually get into a situation where they never see one another.

If you are in a partnership where you derive a lot of joy from your physical relationship, you need to protect that too if you are both leading a pressurized life. You've got to make time to make love. Try not to get in the habit of always going to bed and getting up at different times, or one of you sitting up reading while the other flakes out. You can quickly lose the flow of loving physical contact, and once it has gone out of a partnership it is difficult to bring it back again. Obviously, there are times when exhaustion and worry interrupt physical loving, but if you do value sexual loving as a way of expressing yourself, and sharing your love for each other, let it matter, and give it time.

If your physical loving *has* evaporated in the face of other pressures an embarrassment, almost a feeling of taboo, can grow up between the two of you. If that *has* happened, you can, if you want to, begin again to find a new closeness through a method called 'sensate focusing' described by Sheila Kitzinger in *Woman's Experience of Sex*. You could work on this together, or you might want to talk to a sexual counsellor, to whom you could be referred via your GP or Family Planning Clinic. The most painful and difficult part is probably acknowledging the problem in the first place, and getting over the initial barrier of talking to one another about it and deciding to do something about it.

A loving partnership between a 'working' man and a 'working' woman in this society has other problems as well as shortage of time. Young men are encouraged (by magazines, advertisements, general zeitgeist) to have an essentially physical, *sexual* fantasy about relationships, where young women are encouraged (through the same media) to have a *romantic* fantasy. When the two fantasies don't coincide there can be stress on both sides. This is why it is so urgent to keep the times and opportunities there to be close as whole people. Jean Baker Miller observes in *Towards a New Psychology of Women*:

. . . women stay with, build on, and develop in a context of attachment and affiliation with others. Indeed, women's sense of self [is] very much organized around being able to make and then to maintain affiliation and relationships. Eventually, for many women the threat of disruption of an affiliation is perceived not as just a loss of a relationship but as something closer to a total loss of self. . . .

Looking around you, you will probably see the validity of her observations. In the long term, of course, it would be better to encourage men to develop their emotional awareness so that they do not compartmentalize life and leave you doing all the caring and worrying and 'emotional housework', but until such time as that happens it is probably highly pragmatic to maintain your relationship well, since *you* are probably the one who will suffer loss of self-esteem, confidence, and concentration at work if you don't.

Some women describe their love for their children as even more important than sexual love. They speak of finding the enduring passion for their children more satisfying than the waxing and waning of sexual love. Others find the movement from one rôle to another leaves them confused in their feelings for their children. In no other relationship do you have to be so adaptable, flexible, responsive or responsible. From the symbiosis of pregnancy, and the warm, milky first weeks, to the dual life of work-home, and the child carer or nursery-and-home, you then have to negotiate schools and friends, reading, sums, parties, bullies, lifts to clubs and societies, new freedoms. Surprisingly the small howling bundle metamorphoses more quickly than you would believe possible into a gangling teenager who presents you daily with moral, financial and organizational dilemmas, challenging you with a slight sneer and from a great height, but still deeply hurt if you ever say a cross or sarcastic word.

Just as you have the balancing act off to perfection, your career and home life skilfully and ingeniously poised, the children disappear into lives of their own, without a backward glance. This of course is what you aimed for, that they should eventually be independent, but it's still a shock. You wonder what the struggle was all for, and in bad moments develop real fellow-feeling with King Lear, who was driven mad by an ungrateful offspring. Just when you thought the job was done, the child or children fledged, you realize you have to readjust your times, schedules, rhythms and ambitions to a life with spaces in it where the children used to be. As you work on that, they may have crises and return temporarily for some of your time and attention.

An appreciation of how rich, varied and changeable the love you share with your children can be seems to be the single most important point. Hard though it is to do, working mothers with years of experience emphasize how important it is to value each stage as it happens.

Beth, a gymnastics teacher and mother of a girl and a boy now both in secondary school, speaks with regret of how she 'wished away' the early years of their lives:

I was always thinking how much easier it would be when they got onto the next stage. When they could only sit up, I longed for them to crawl, and when they crawled I longed for them to walk. I thought everything would get much easier when they went to school – it wasn't really. Now I wish I could have those times back again and not hurry them through it all.

Adèle, studying law while her third child was still an infant warns of the trap of seeing children all the time in a negative light:

Adam and I both missed out on a lot when he was tiny because I was frazzled about the logistics of what I was trying to do and I got into the habit of seeing him as a problem I had to solve and not as a person. When he was about 18 months old I suddenly realized his life was racing on and I wasn't allowing him or me a chance to get close to each other. I just thought, he didn't ask to be born, and he and I have got to matter to each other, I've got to stop manoeuvring him into as small a space as possible. It wasn't a matter of time, it was mentally and emotionally, I just had to acknowledge I want my job, I want to pass my exams, but I want him and me to be good friends too. We've managed a lot better since I realized that although I found working it out painful and confusing.

Sometimes a dramatic event changes your perspective. Karen has four children, widely spaced in age, and a job in administration. She was feeling particularly cross and overwhelmed by them all one Saturday morning. 'I specifically remember wishing I hadn't so many kids,' she says, 'when my four-year-old son came rushing in from the garden – his mouth was trying to scream, but no sound was coming out. He then went blue round the mouth and collapsed. He had stopped breathing. A wasp flew out of his mouth.' She realized that he had taken a bite out of an apple which had had a wasp sitting on it. The wasp, stuck in his mouth, had stung him towards the back of the throat, and his trachaea had closed up where the sting swelled up:

We scooped up him and the baby. Our hands were all fingers and thumbs. We couldn't open the front door, or get the keys in the car without a lot of fumbling. I couldn't think of anything to do except rest him face down over my knee and massage his spine. I was aghast at how your children could be lost, in a second, just like that. I don't believe in God, but I prayed. On the way to Casualty he started to breathe again. . . .

Shaking at the memory she says; 'It never occurred to me that anything really awful could happen to *my* children. It made me think I must never think "I wish I didn't have them" ever again, because it made me realize how easily any of them could be gone.'

Alice, her youngest child (of three) about to leave home at nineteen, says:

She's gone for a job in another city today, and I hope she gets it and moves out, but it isn't a simple feeling. I shall miss her, she's been very good company, these last few years, and I'm a bit wary of what it will be like not to be a mother of someone in my house any more. But on the whole, I think if she comes back and says she hasn't got the job I shall be fed up at the thought of her being around any longer. I'm ready to move into the next phase now.

Sinead seems to sum it all up by saying:

There are a million phases in your relationship with your children. All you can do is to take them one at a time. Always remember you've never got it all wrapped up and tidy, because it never is. Whenever you have a happy time together, mentally underline it in your memory, it will help you withstand everything else you go through together.

Love shared with friends, and with your extended family, can sustain you and your children, and, if you have one, your partner. Forming a partnership and then having children certainly sifts through and sorts out old friends. Old established friends, if they have any possessive feelings about you, will be challenged by and jealous of a loving partnership, and there is often an initial shake-out of friends at that stage. Later on friends without children may be slow to adjust the kind of socializing they want to have with you in a way that is considerate of your children. They may also be jealous of your children, or feel their own way of life challenged or compromised by you becoming parents, so there is often another shake-out at this stage. However, real alliances, friendships that grow as your life changes, new people met through work and at the antenatal clinic, and so forth, bring variety and breadth of experience and humour into your existence.

Unless you find cooking positively relaxing, this is not the right bit of your life for throwing elaborate dinner parties. Informal parties that take minimum preparation are better because then you have the energy left to enjoy the company, which is, after all, the object of the exercise. Make a rule of thumb to have two social events a month (or a week, or a year! or whatever you feel you need) and then make a small patch of time each week to organize them. Otherwise meetings and briefs and deadlines and overtime will roll time relentlessly on past you, and you'll suddenly realize it's six months since you met with friends or members of your extended family. If these people are important to you, make sure you fit them in, and don't lose touch.

If you are lucky enough to have a rewarding job or to work in a lively team, love for your colleagues will have been one of your main incentives for 'getting back' to work. This is using the word 'love' in its widest sense, meaning warm feelings towards other like-minded people. For many women, the loss of this easy-going love among equal adults is the most shocking loss upon giving up work. The restoration of this love when you go back to work is a great joy.

It can, however, create difficulties. Sam describes her emotions a couple of weeks after returning to her work on a newspaper after several years out of journalism while her children were very small:

I fell in love with a colleague, briefly, but I was taken aback by it. Both he and I are happily married and he never knew how I felt – I used to be overwhelmed by fantasies about running away with him. In retrospect I think I was just intoxicated by being my own person again, by people treating me like someone who wasn't just somebody's mother. I was bowled over by other people's response to me and my response to them, although I should think to them it was all very ordinary. It loomed large to me and felt all very out of hand until I got used to it, which took about six months.

Her point illustrates just how interesting and attractive the company of adult colleagues is if you have been separated from it for some time. It may be worth thinking about avoiding making any radical changes in partnerships for a little while after returning to work, in case disturbing new feelings are more to do with the excitement of returning than anything else. After a few months you might find you veer from quite liking to cordially loathing your workmates again, just as you did before!

Finally, you may want some space in your life for some kind of spiritual love. 'Spiritually speaking' says Ginny Babcock, heroine of Lisa Alther's *Kinflicks*, 'I'm an easy lay'. Any of us who have felt a bit empty emotionally may ruefully recognize her predicament. 'Fringe' religious sects may prey on people in periods of low self-esteem, who are temporarily lacking in a structure for their values and systems of living, and it might be useful to notice the times when we might be vulnerable to unscrupulous cults. Nonetheless we may need to have a spiritual element in our lives that can be fulfilled. It might be fulfilled in your work. Nadia, a midwife, says of her job: 'You never get used to it, it never gets stale. No matter how many times I see a baby being born I just marvel at it and think what a miracle it is.' Your spiritual experience might lie in listening to music, dancing, or singing, or taking a chance to walk in the country, to marvel at trees and plants, the sky and the sea. It might be in prayer, or meditation, in growing flowers, in music, in studying a physical discipline.

If you do feel empty inside, or jaded, or un-centred, maybe your spiritual needs are not being met. Maybe you could think about what has in the past given you a sense of equilibrium, of being part of a spiritual whole. Some of those things are probably free and not too time-consuming and could be brought back into your life without too much trouble.

In this apparently irrational hunger, the heart has its reasons, and its reasons are keeping alive your whole self in all its aspects, however busy and full your schedule may be.

Further Reading

Boston Women's Health Collective *Our Bodies Ourselves*. Penguin 1978.

Chernin, Kim *The Hungry Self*. Virago 1989.

Dale, Barbara, and Roeber, Johanna *Exercises for Childbirth*. Century 1982.

Davidson, John, and Davidson, Farida *Natural Fertility Awareness*. C. W. Daniel 1986.

Dickson, Ann *A Woman in Your Own Right*. Quartet 1982.

Kenton, Leslie *Raw Energy.* Century 1985.

Kitzinger, Sheila *Woman's Experience of Sex*. Dorling Kindersley 1983.

Last, Nella *Nella Last's War*. Sphere Books 1983.

Macleod, Sheila *The Art of Starvation*. Virago 1981.

Miller, Jean Baker *Towards a New Psychology of Women*. Penguin 1978.

Piercey, Marge *A Woman on The Edge of Time*. Women's Press 1979.

Shilt, Randy *And The Band Played On*. Penguin 1988.

Sivananda Yoga Group *The Book of Yoga.* Ebury Press 1983.

Useful Addresses

Networking Addresses

The Women and Training Group Hewmar House, 120 London Road, Gloucester GLI 3PL.

Women Returners Network Contact Secretary to the Principal, Chelmsford AEC, Patching Hall Lane, Chelmsford, Essex CMI 4DB.

European Women's Management Development Network Valerie Hammond (President), Ashridge Management College, Berkhamsted, Herts HP4 INS.

Helplines

Frontliners 01 831 0330

AIDS Helpline 0800 567123

Gingerbread 35 Wellington Street, London WC2; 01 240 0953

TRANX 25a Masons Avenue, Wealdstone, Harrow, Middlesex. Tel. 01 427 2065, Mon-Fri 10 am–4 pm; 01 427 2787 24-hour answering service.

Tranxline (Involuntary Addicts Support Group): 24 Hardman Street, Liverpool L1 9AX

Alcoholics Anonymous local branch in phone book.

Samaritans local branch in phone book.

Index